Wilderness Dreams

Wilderness Dreams

JACK BOUDREAU

CAITLIN PRESS INC. 2003

Published by Caitlin Press Inc.
Box 2387
Prince George BC V2N 2S6

Cover and interior design by Roger Handling / Terra Firma Digital Arts
Index by Kathy Plett
Map by Rich Rawling

National Library of Canada Cataloguing in Publication Data

Boudreau, Jack, 1933-
Wilderness dreams / Jack Boudreau

 Includes index
ISBN 1-894759-00-1

1. Pioneers – British Columbia – Cariboo Region – Biography. 2. Frontier and pioneer life – British Columbia – Cariboo region. 3. Bowden family. 4. Bowden, Clara.
5. Cariboo region (B.C.) – Biography. I. Title
FC3845.C3Z48 2003   971.1'7503'0922   C2003-910848-1
F1089.C3B8 2003

Caitlin Press Inc. wishes to acknowledge the financial support of the Canada
Council for the Arts, the Britishs Columbia Arts Council and the Book Publishing
Industry Development Program of the Canadian Heritage Department for its
publishing program.

Acknowledgements

First off I wish to thank the extended Bowden family for their assistance.

To the people who assisted me in one way or another I must thank Helen, Steve and David Wlasitz; also Steve Buba and Eric Klaubauf for their expertise and assistance on my computer problems, many of which are self-inflicted.

To Quesnel's *Cariboo Observer*, I offer thanks for the liberal use of their newspaper to check stories and dates.

Books by Jack Boudreau

Crazy Man's Creek
Grizzly Bear Mountain
Mountains, Campfires and Memories
Wilderness Dreams

Contents

FOREWORD

My first meeting with Hap (Ted) and Clara Bowden occurred because of a pilot named Don Redden. Don, in turn, had met the Bowdens in 2001 because a man at Transport Canada had phoned him to advise that an elderly couple had built an airplane and needed someone to test fly it for them. When Don learned that the couple were in their seventies he got a mental picture of a plane with its wingtips touching the ground. But he investigated further and on checking, found that they had done a magnificent job with the aircraft. Several times throughout the following year Don kept telling me that I simply had to meet these people, because as he put it, "I've never met people like this in my life; in fact, I didn't even believe they existed."

Don finally got the point home to me, so in October 2002 I went with him to the Bowden home along the Quesnel River. Once there, it didn't take very long for me to realize that Don's assessment was not only true, it was also an understatement. After listening to many of their stories and seeing the supporting photographic proof, I told Clara and Hap that I would be delighted to write a book about their most interesting lives and they jumped at the chance.

The lives these two people have lived and the sum total of their adventures defy logic. Even today, at the ages of 76 and 80, Clara and Hap live lives that are filled with one adventure after another. At a time when many people have given up on life at the age of sixty or seventy, these two people can be an inspiration to all. They prove the old adage that we are only as old as we feel and the best way to avoid feeling old is to do, do, and do some more. Always the comedian, Hap says that a man has to be careful when he tries to feel young because he can get his face slapped.

Hap's adventures, first during World War Two, and later, his prospecting trip into the far north form a powerful opening to a life of constant adventure. The prospecting trip into Johanson Lake was recorded in a diary he took along and it tells how he and a friend left Vancouver for a prolonged stay in the wilderness. When they returned three months later they were 20 pounds lighter and a lot more worldly wise.

There can be no doubt that Hap was always his own man; I believe this yearning to be his own boss was what drove him to work so hard for so many years when he could have worked half the number of hours for someone else. One gentleman who knew Hap back in the 50s told me, "He was a stubborn son of a gun but I have to admit that he was a first class guide." I countered by saying that a person had to be stubborn and resolute or they simply would not have been able to face the challenges and disappointments that confronted the Bowdens so often during their first years in the forests.

Clara's story is unique in its own right. An exceptionally beautiful young lady, she gave up her life in the city and followed Hap's dreams into the wilderness of BC. There were to be many tough days in her future, such as staying alone many miles from anyone while Hap was occupied at different projects. But she carried the load with much stoicism and an upbeat outlook on life that we all can learn from. Few people have impressed me as much as Clara has.

Clara, thankfully, kept diaries for about 40 years and I am proud that she trusted them to my care. I thoroughly enjoyed reading of their many adventures during the years that they purchased their own land and started the Diamond B Bar Ranch. Just a few years later they built and ran Cariboo Mountain Outfitters in the mountainous area east of Quesnel, BC. Regrettably, 12 years of her diaries were lost when a fire destroyed the cookhouse on their guideline.

It seems so strange to read about her trials and aspirations, not to mention the manner in which she faced whatever life threw at her. It was an enormous undertaking for me to attempt to read the 40 years of adventures that are covered in her many diaries. In many of the books the inks had faded or run and were difficult to impossible to discern. For a time I thought that I had bitten off more than I could chew, but I hung in there and after a period of three months, finally turned the last page.

After Clara and Hap guided hunters for 25 years, they decided a change was overdue so they purchased a commercial fishing boat and spent three years on the ocean. Then it was back to their beloved wilderness way of life along the Quesnel River where they spent many years prospecting.

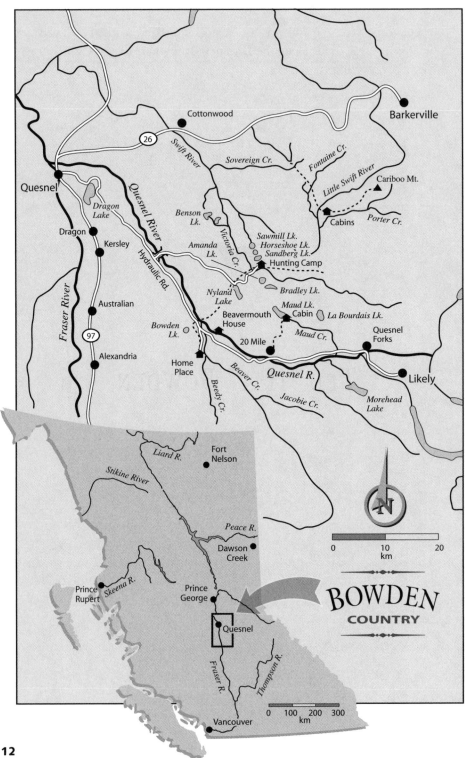

Cottonwood

Barkerville

26

Swift River

Sovereign Cr.

Fontaine Cr.

Little Swift River

Cariboo Mt.

Quesnel

Dragon Lake

Dragon

Kersley

Quesnel River

Hydraulic Rd.

Fraser River

97

Australian

Alexandria

Benson Lk.

Amanda Lk.

Victoria Cr.

Sawmill Lk.
Horseshoe Lk.
Sandberg Lk.

Hunting Camp

Bradley Lk.

Nyland Lake

Maud Lk.

Cabin

La Bourdais Lk.

Beavermouth House

20 Mile

Maud Cr.

Quesnel Forks

Bowden Lk.

Home Place

Beaver Cr.

Quesnel R.

Likely

Beedy Cr.

Jacobie Cr.

Morehead Lake

Cabins

Porter Cr.

Liard R.

Fort Nelson

Stikine River

Peace R.

Dawson Creek

Prince Rupert

Skeena R.

Prince George

Quesnel

Fraser R.

Thompson R.

Vancouver

N

0   10   20
km

BOWDEN
COUNTRY

0 100 200 300
km

CHAPTER ONE
TED "HAP" BOWDEN

Daniel Teddy Robert Bowden, known to all his friends as Hap or Ted, was born in Ponoka, Alberta in 1922. When he was two years old his family moved to the Fraser Valley in BC. At the age of 15 Hap rode the rods out to the Prairies to try his hand at taking in the harvest. At Lloydminister he stayed for a spell with his half-brother, Les Gates–a boxer with 247 fights to his credit.

Hap with his half-brother Les Gates on left. Les was a boxer with 247 fights. 1940.

Hap spent the summer working on a farm where he was forced to sleep under a haystack, as there was no room for him in the sod house. When the harvest was over, he headed back toward Vancouver and along the way had a strange experience. He stopped at a roadside café and went inside and purchased a bottle of pop. As he walked out the door, he felt what he thought was a hand on his shoulder. He whirled about to behold a black bear standing up right beside him. At that instant the owner shouted, "Give him the pop!" Hap did as he was directed and then watched as the bear guzzled all the pop, down to the last drop. Did the owner replace the bottle of pop, you ask? Not a chance. That was the price Hap had to pay for his first meeting with a tame bear.

The following year, 1938, Hap went to a hiring agency where he was hired to split wood for a wood burning cold-decking machine. This was in the woods at Port Renfrew. Later, he spent several years working at Port McNeil. During this time he worked nine months without any time off. Within a few short years he mastered most of the jobs, including a stint as high rigger.

Hap showing off changing blocks. 1941.

Perhaps Hap's most vivid memory of those days concerned a terrible accident that occurred when they were loading logs on flatcars. A train would regularly spot 11 empty flatcars into the siding to be loaded with logs, but on that occasion they inserted 12 cars. A one and a quarter inch cable was attached to the first car so that the donkey engine could move them along as each car was loaded with logs. Because the 12 cars were moved in, the cable hit the end of the drum and broke, causing the cable to snap back with great force striking three men who were standing along the brow log. One man was thrown through the air and received fractured ribs that penetrated his lungs; he later died. A second man was hit across the knee and though his leg was split open for about ten inches, he tended himself and shouted for Hap to assist the third man who was terribly injured. This man had been hit just below the knees with the result that one leg was severed and the other leg just held by a cord. Hap grabbed some rags off the machine and rushed in to apply tourniquets to the man's legs. This man survived, although he got gangrene and had to have both legs amputated.

Hap has many memories from his logging days on the coast. Such as the time the crew adopted and started feeding a black bear. This was not a smart move, because the next day this same bear found and

Donkey Engine. Arrow points to where the cable killed the man.

ate all their lunches. As is so often the case this bear had to be destroyed a short time later.

Another memory concerned a fight he got into at a dance. As they fell to the ground together, his rival must have believed he was Mike Tyson, because he sank his teeth into Hap's cheek. They wrestled around a bit until Hap got free, only to have the fellow bite him again in a different spot. Desperately Hap searched for a way out, and suddenly his hand touched what turned out to be a full bottle of beer in the man's pocket. With all his strength Hap struck the man across the head with the bottle, then felt him relax. Unconscious, he was taken to the hospital where he soon recovered. As for Hap, when he re-entered the hall the boss approached him and asked why he had struck the man with a bottle. Hap simply turned his head to display the two bites on his face and the boss stated, "The son of a bitch bit you. Good! He got what was coming to him." The incident was never mentioned again.

Hap joined the army in 1942 and already his sense of humour was obvious. When asked who should be notified in case of his death, he offered, "Probably the morgue would be best." Hap quickly learned that people in officious positions are often short on humour.

Hap went into training with a command communications unit at Red Deer, Alberta, and then went overseas where he served as a dispatch rider. The motorcycle proved more hazardous than the logging business, though, with the result that he was the victim of more than 40 spills during his stay in Europe. One such spill almost tore his left thumb off, with the result that he ended up with a small pension.

His closest brush with disaster during his time in the military came while he was attempting to change oil in a jeep. As he worked away he was shocked when a sniper's bullet barely missed him and struck the ground right beside him. The guilty party was quickly taken into custody.

Hap in Germany, 1944. Medals were taken from German prisoners.

Hap took part in the Battle of the Bulge at Caen right after the invasion of Normandy and then stayed on for two years in the army of occupation. One of his most memorable duties was serving in the Canadian unit that went to the relief of the German horror camp at Belson where they liberated many living skeletons in the closing days of the war. On his return from overseas Hap experienced severe health problems that placed him in the hospital for several months.

After four years in the military, life in the logging camps lost its appeal, so Hap turned to prospecting for a change of style. This urge for adventure almost cost him his life.

In March 1947 *The Vancouver Sun* noted:

"The migration northward has begun, to hunt gold in the Goldway Peak strike area. Today two Vancouver athletes are off to Johanson Creek, 300 miles north of Goldway, in the heart of a heavily mineralized section of northern British Columbia. They are Roy 'Rusty' Gates, well known to wrestling fans, and Ted Bowden, amateur boxer.

"The story of the strike in the Sustat and Johanson Lake areas was revealed for the first time to the outside world by The *Vancouver Sun's* Headless Valley expedition. Queries have been reaching *The Sun* office from men all over the United States and Canada who are interested in looking for gold . . ."

Hap and Roy Gates ready for the trip, March, 1947.

Rusty and Hap went into this venture with great vigor. While Rusty took a crash course in mineralogy, Hap set to work gathering the equipment necessary for the journey.

During my interviews with Hap he made mention of several half-brothers. Always the comedian, he asked if I knew the definition of a half-brother. When I admitted that I didn't, he explained, "A half-brother is a guy with only one testicle." I didn't bother asking for the definition of a half-sister.

Hap kept a diary of their expedition and it started shortly before they left. He noted that he had sold his car and spent several days shopping, hoping they didn't forget anything of significance. He mentioned having a camera and lots of film, and stated that they had to be sure that one of the rifles would be dependable.

Finally on March 10th, after buying another gun, 32.20 cartridges and some maps, they caught a freight train and "rode the rods" as so many people did in those days. Hap pointed out that it sure was hot in his heavy underwear and mackinaw pants. As they sat atop the catwalk above a boxcar they watched for a long time until the lights of Vancouver faded away into darkness. During that time they discussed the odds of their returning someday flush with gold from faraway places.

On March 11th, after having a meal in a hobo jungle, they caught another drag out of Kamloops. The bulls (police) saw them boarding the train but didn't bother them, probably glad to see them leaving their town. Hap next noted, "God, the sage sure smells nice here in the dry belt." As they neared Ashcroft the temperature began dropping and suddenly they found it was snowing.

When the men reached Red Pass Junction they were forced to change trains again. This meant camping out beneath the stars. Hap noted in his diary, "We heard the wolves proper last night; after the shivers stopped running through us, Roy and I were convinced that they were really hungry."

The next morning, after a feast of coffee, ham and doughnuts, the world looked a bit brighter. Hap claimed that the women were sure sociable, even inviting them up to their homes. He then added, "Of course we didn't accept."

Now do you believe what I say about Hap's sense of humor?

Hap and Roy wandered over to the railroad roundhouse after breakfast and spent some time talking to the fireman who told them when the next train would arrive heading west. This gave them a chance to catch up on some much needed sleep in the warmth of the building. By four that afternoon they were in Prince George where, with their heavy woolen clothes and moccasins, they "felt so conspicuous." They changed clothing and made their way to a café where, with T-bone steak on order, they got the jukebox wound up with "The Jersey Bounce." With that Hap wrote, "Everything is under control." The next entry read, "Prince George is a nice little town; had two beers apiece; sure is a lovely night; beautiful sunset."

After a good nights sleep in the roundhouse, the men caught the passenger train bound for Hazelton. But not the coach, rather they crawled onto the back of the tender where, because they had neglected to wear their mackinaws, they almost froze to death. As the train rolled along belching smoke and steam, the engineer spotted a large boulder on the tracks and brought the train to a screeching halt. Then the jig was up, because the crew could not remove the rock. Hap and Roy rushed out and helped, and by the combined effort, got the train on its way again. Perhaps because they so freely offered their assistance, the young men were allowed to ride in comfort for the remainder of the journey to Smithers.

As soon as they descended the train, a resident accosted them and asked for a bottle of rum. Then he informed them that they never rolled up the sidewalks in Smithers. Another way of saying that it was always party time around there.

After a good night's sleep, the men went to a café where they ordered bacon and eggs. Hap noted, "The jukebox is staggering to the rhythm of "That Chicken Is Too Young To Fry." And after the meal was finished he added, "Roy thinks the waitress is kind of cute; she's okay in my opinion, too."

When Hap went to pay the bill, he pulled out a $100 bill but could not get it cashed. It seemed as though these people had never seen a bill that large before. Everyone simply stared at them.

Finally on March 17th they arrived in Hazelton where their real adventure was about to begin. It is my belief that if they had even a glimpse of what the future was to hold they would quickly have retraced their steps to Vancouver.

Hap had been very impressed with the town of Smithers, especially with the scenic view of the rivers and mountains, but he was by no means so impressed with the town of Hazelton. The people stared at them as if they had not seen a stranger in years, as well, they asked too many questions. As Hap and Roy waited for their supplies to arrive, their concern grew, as the rising temperature meant that the ice was rotting on the Skeena River. At this point they decided to splurge, so they got a hotel room. Hap noted, "Gosh! It's nice to have a good wash and a lovely bed, white sheets and all, and we also had a big pork dinner tonight."

The following day the men decided to kill time by helping people haul freight. That evening Hap stated that he was beginning to like the place. Perhaps the next statement he made gives away what influenced him, "Johnny Marshall just introduced me to his daughter, Betty; what a surprise I got; I didn't even think he was married."

Several of the Indians and trappers they talked with impressed upon them that they needed a dog team and that they had better hit the trail soon because the ice along the river and in the canyons didn't look so good.

By March 20th the cash was running low so the men moved into a garage to sleep. After noting that they had bought their first dog, named Dick, for $10, Hap mentioned that he had never seen so many children in such a small place, and suggested that he knew what they did for entertainment around there.

Their supplies arrived on March 22nd, and by that time – thanks to the help of others – they had several collars and harnesses for their dogs. Two days later they were on their way up the Skeena River with their sleigh loaded to the limit. That evening Hap noted, "We had bad luck today. We caught a ride with a truck for a short distance and one of our dogs jumped out and got ran over; we had to shoot it. We camped beside an Indian hut and they invited us in for stew; it was the first thing we had to eat since breakfast and I sure went for it. We bought another dog for $5 so now we have no money for flour when we get to Bear Lake."

The day of the 25th the men covered 10 miles (16km) and the dogs were done in. To make matters even worse, they had to be on the trail by 4 o'clock because the top layer of ice went soft before noon. Hap wrote, "Roy is frying bacon; God! It sure smells good."

The danger involved in traveling before daylight was demonstrated the next morning when they nearly lost their sleigh in a crevice. When they made camp after an eight-mile trek the dogs were so exhausted that they appeared to be dead. After a meal, the men put

Hap Bowden on the Skeena River
March, 1947.

on their snowshoes and went hunting for moose, grouse or rabbits, or anything that would add to the food supply. They found where a moose had been killed but could not find the cache, if there was one. That night they were serenaded by a pack of wolves, but the barking of the dogs kept them in the distance.

On the 27th, utterly exhausted from fighting the soft snow, they passed what they figured was the Kiskigas River. When they made camp, these young men learned a bit about the nature of dogs when they petted one of them in appreciation for a job well done. Instantly the other dogs attacked the one they had petted and they had a major dogfight on their hands.

When they checked their progress on the map, they were shocked to find that they had only covered three miles, yet Hap stated that he had not been so hungry in many years.

March 28th was a really tough day. The snow was like sugar and the dogs got so tired that they flopped down on the snow and refused to move for a while. In total they had to make two portages wearing snowshoes to support themselves.

On the 29th Hap noted that they had been bothered all night by a lynx, but that they couldn't get a shot at it. By morning, when they tried to make breakfast, the bannock was frozen as well as their socks. The campfire had melted itself down four feet into the snow so they didn't get much heat from it. Even worse, Hap noted that once they were back on the trail they were looking forward to another "hell of a portage."

By the afternoon of March 30th they had completed the portage and had arrived totally exhausted at an Indian cabin, which they figured was 80 miles from Hazelton. Here they were in for a special surprise because they found moose meat that had been left in a cache. It was just what they had been praying and hunting for to feed themselves and their dogs. Hap wrote, "Just had my first feed of moose meat; God! It was good."

The next day was Sunday, so the boys and the dogs rested up. Repairs were made to the sled and Roy made a batch of bread to take on their journey. After inspecting the bread Hap mentioned, "The bread Roy made is heavy but it sure looks good."

Again Hap's humour showed itself when he noted, "Roy pulled an April Fool's Day joke by going through the ice. Then our dog, Bob, ate a pound of lard. Snuffy, the youngest dog got sick, probably from eating too much dried fish. Roy sure looks funny in his underwear standing on some boughs by the fire, but the fire sure feels good."

Entries like this were common in the diary; it seemed that each day brought problems anew.

April 2nd – "Got up this morning to find our socks and pants frozen stiff, and on top of that we had a hard time getting a fire going. We got up at four o'clock, ate mush, bread and syrup. We went two miles and then hit the Kuldo Canyon. It took us all day to get by it and we risked our lives in several places. Once the toboggan was hanging by a rope but we got it down all right. After dinner we covered about four miles until we came to a place where the ice was out. This meant we had to travel along the edge of the river or go back through the bush, which is almost impossible with the big load we have. Lots of moose sign but we're too tired to go after them. Hard to find a good place to camp now because the banks are so steep."

Some days were so crammed with adventure that I will just relate directly from Hap's diary.

April 3rd – "Got up at four, ate, harnessed dogs and traveled good for three hours, then ran into a blinding snowstorm. Roy fell through the ice with the outfit on top of him; good thing the water wasn't deep. Then I fell in at Guish Creek while I was trying to find a place to ford it. The ice gave away and I fell right into the main current. It was a good thing I had taken my pack and rifle off. I just made it out because the cold water had paralyzed my legs already. We kept going and covered 25 miles when we reached a steep mountain at 3:15 p.m. We climbed it and found a cabin. There was a cache of fuel and food here and we sure needed a good night of sleep."

The next morning they moved on and soon realized that they were a long way from the top of the mountain. Hap had been nursing an injury to his hand that he had sustained before the trip, and now it became infected with soreness under his armpit. He made a poultice for it and hoped for the best. Roy had a problem of his own to deal with because one of the dogs bit his hand right to the bone.

On April 5th Hap wrote, "Twelve days on the trail. We thought we were over the mountain but still a long way to go; it took us four days to cover sixteen miles. We stumbled onto a small cabin; the dogs found it. The roof was partly caved in and it was so small we couldn't stand up in it, but there was wood there so we spent the night."

April 6th –"We had a tough day again today; made four miles. One dog tried to get away. He thought the hill was too steep to climb so he tried to swim the river. I fired some shots in front of him so he turned and came back. I had to get in the river, pull him out and help him up the bank. Then we got a fire going to get him back to life."

April 7th–"We made about 15 miles today; passed around one bad crevice in a canyon. Met three white trappers coming out with their furs. They wanted to know the price of furs and we wanted to know what the ice was like upriver. They told us that the big mountain we had come over was known as Poison Mountain."

Hap at camp, 1947.

April 8th –"Been fighting a snow storm all day. Fell in the river toboggan and all. Had to quit and make a fire. Made about nine miles today. Roy is brewing mush for the dogs as we are almost out of dog food. We may have to stop a day to hunt but we hate to lose that much traveling time."

April 9th –"Just burned my hand trying to cook mush for the dogs in a gold pan. We made about 15 miles today. Wolves and a bear circled our camp all night; they had a very nice trail worn around it. Wolves must be awful big by the size of their tracks. We haven't seen one yet but the dogs sure let you know when they are there. We are at the mouth of Squingula River, only five miles to the Sustut River. The axe was tied on the toboggan and I cut my hand to the bone on it. We are sure getting good with the axe."

April 10th –"The wolves kept us up all night. We had to tie one of the dogs up to keep it from getting killed as it is always ready to fight. We made the Sustut River okay and came through two bad canyons. We found an old trapper's cabin; no stove but I rigged one up, as there are stovepipes here. Roy hunted for rabbits but no stew tonight."

April 11th started out on a bright note as Hap noted, "First blood. We got a fine bull moose traveling down the ice on the other side of the river. I hit him behind the hump and Roy broke one front leg. He was nice and fat . . . We just finished the best feed of this trip so far. I am so full I can hardly write. The dogs are chewing on the bones. We are going to take 150 pounds with us and leave the rest in a tree for anyone that comes along."

The young adventurers got off to an early start on the 12th, but eight miles along they lost the whole issue through the ice. Hap wrote, "Roy was lucky to get off, but our flour, raisins and some of our grub got wet. Then we had to travel two miles through the snow to our camp. It sure is hell with the snowshoes on and dogs that are tired . . . I ate about three pounds of steak – no kidding. I have never had such a ravenous appetite."

The snow turned to rain, so for the next two days the lads just lazed around camp, slept and gorged themselves on moose meat. Only in retrospect did they fully realize just how trail weary they had become. As they whiled away the time in camp, they studied their mineral books as well as a book on edible vegetation. As we shall see later, the vegetation thing would come back to bite them.

April 15th was the 22nd day on the trail. Hap wrote, "We woke up with a start as the dogs were all barking at a wolverine. It was only 15 yards from our camp and there was still smoke rising from our campfire that didn't seem to scare it, but it sure took off when I got up. There was a beautiful sunrise and it sure made you feel like a free man when it came up over the mountain and reflected off the river ice. We passed one creek and two ledges; one place we unloaded, tied the toboggan to a tree and pushed it along with the open river right below us. We had to quit at 11:30 because the dogs and us were all in."

The next evening Hap wrote, "We only made about two miles today. We went over one small mountain and across the river, then back across the river again on a flow of ice around an ice cliff. Roy went ahead with the .22 to try to get four mallards, while I put a pot on the campfire waiting for the supreme feast, but no luck. Instead I ate the equivalent of 24 eggs and Roy ate 12, so you can imagine the appetite a man gets on the trail."

By April 17th the lads and their dogs had used up all the moose meat and had started on some jerky they got from the Indians. It was tough slogging through the snow, with the result that they only covered a mile and a half that day. In the distance they could see a mountain range that they took to be the Connelly Range.

On April 18th Hap noted, "We put in a hell of a day, deep snow with the toboggan going through and us going through with our snowshoes. We have to travel the banks all the way because there is no ice. We can't understand it aside from the fact that we are too late. We passed Bear River and one creek, and then made a bridge over an ice flow. We made three or four miles at the most and we are all in. We had a big feed of hotcakes for dinner as we had to quit the jerky because it was giving us the runs. The mosquitoes are out now doing their part. We are downhearted but still not discouraged. I guess we will have to put a wheel on our toboggan soon."

On the 19th the diary continued, "Well, we are still here in the canyon. Another big chunk of ice went out forcing us to go over another sheer cliff. I went to get water with the snowshoes on and sank right to my waist with every step. It sure plays you out. Can't go anywhere; just have to sit tight and wait till the snow either freezes or melts. Had our first feed of beans today and more hotcakes."

The 20th started out in an unusual way. Hap had soaked some dried moose meat and intended to mix in a bunch of powdered eggs to make it more palatable, but when he went to get the eggs he had left unattended he found that the dog, Killer Bob, had eaten the five dozen powdered eggs, wax paper and all. Hap caught the dog and a fight ensued during which Killer was chastised, to put it mildly.

Things brightened considerably, though, when Roy shot a bull moose just above their camp. Once again they thought that all were in for a treat. When Hap fried a steak for himself he found it so unpalatable that he couldn't eat it, but the dogs pigged out to such an extent they spent the evening on the snow, groaning.

April 21st dawned clear and cold, so after a breakfast of rice the lads were on the trail. Hap wrote, "We spent three and a half hours getting over a steep bluff. It was just one portage after another. In one steep spot a rock I dislodged almost hit Roy. In another spot we had to build a pole bridge and while we were trying to get the dogs over, the axe was accidentally kicked into the river and lost. Fortunately for us, Roy had found a small axe at an old cabin and it will have to do the job. We only made about two miles today; it was the worst day on the trail so far."

A trapper's small cabin, 1947.

Just how much these two explorers pushed their luck was detailed on the 22nd. "Up at four and had hotcakes for breakfast, then we hit the trail. We traveled hard through the canyons for about three hours and then hit open country around Sayia Creek about seven miles from where we had camped. We had to cross the river [Sustut] on the ice and we both knew it was a gamble. I figured if I ran fast and pulled the toboggan that I could make it across and I did. But Roy was still on the other side with two packs and both rifles. I urged him on and he made a run for and made it – all the way up to his neck in the river. He managed to get the gear and guns on the ice and I made it out to where I threw a rope to him. He got out and we saved the gear as well . . . He sure looks funny standing by the fire in his underwear."

The next evening, sitting by a fire Hap noted, "We have been wading the river up to our ass. We made four miles today through real tough going and we were almost at the Asitka River when we were cut off completely by a sheer wall. We had to wade the river and got all the supplies over, but the dogs will have to swim in the morning. We have gambled the outfit, the dogs and our lives a hundred times in the last 30 days. The frozen North is well named."

April 24th ended with these comments, "We had to cross the river again. It froze but not enough to hold us up on the snow, so we had to stop at 8:15 a.m. It was really tough, dogs pulling and both of us pushing. It is sure good to be off the Sustut, as this Asitka River is smaller and less dangerous. Sun is shining on the mountain; sure is pretty."

For the next two days the lads were trapped in camp at the mouth of the Asitka. Almost out of food for the dogs, they tried hunting but could not travel in the rotten snow. Roy managed to get a fool hen, which was quickly devoured by men and dogs.

April 27th – "We left in soft snow, up to our necks, and we only made a half-mile. We both agree it was the toughest day yet, but we had to move because the ice in the canyon is going out and we can't go back even if we want to. We got out the last of the beans and the flour is almost gone. The dogs are on half rations so they will eat tomorrow, after that we may have to kill one of them. We are both starving hungry."

It was raining hard the morning of the 28th so the lads only made half a mile. Their meal consisted of some milk and raisons. "God they taste good." Hap observed.

Over the next two days they covered about two miles, sometimes having to carry everything up over steep spots along the river. The water had risen making it more hazardous to ford. On May 1st Hap wrote, "It froze last night and the water went down. When I got up I couldn't believe it but the ice was gone; there was just open water and we were on the wrong side of the river. We had to ford it, so I went first and fell face down in the water. We moved everything over and then packed the toboggan last. Roy is making saddles for the dogs now. We sure hate to leave the toboggan as we wanted to use the boards and nails later."

The entry for May 2nd was even more depressing, "God! What a life. Got no sleep last night because of back trouble. Spent too many hours in the water, I guess. We had trouble today and made only one mile under pathetic conditions. We are not throwing away anything we might need so our packs are very heavy. We hope to do better tomorrow when the dogs have adjusted to their packs. They are having a hell of a time in the brush, and it is marvelous what they go through and the loads they carry. We have to help each other along."

That night was obviously spent in a bad spot because they sat by a campfire all night. Hap wrote, "We made two and a half miles today and had to ford the river three times. The dogs were marvelous; the way they carry over 35 pounds each. It is something to watch, and the ones that have been broke to packing don't seem to mind at all. Snuffy is a little scared at times and he seems to be getting very thin. We passed an Indian camp today, not more than two days old. I guess he's trapping here somewhere. All told we have enough grub for three weeks."

May 4th started out with a good crust on the snow but after fording the river three times the lads complained of frozen legs. What made it even tougher was that they had to carry the dogs' packs across the river for fear that they would drown with the packs on. After a four and a half-mile trek, they found a good place to camp. Some of their flour got wet with the result that there was only enough for another week. As well, they ate up the last of the beans for their evening meal.

On May 5th the entry read, "I am sitting by the fire waiting for Roy to come along. He has a heavier pack than me. We have made a good seven miles today. The dogs did great this morning and had no trouble in the brush. They sure can travel fast with a big load on the hard snow. While I made a feed out of flour, raisins and eggs, Roy went ahead looking for the trail but he couldn't find it."

A feeling of elation swept through the lads on May 6th when they found the trail. Hap wrote, "Good God! We finally hit the trail; I was so happy I could have screamed. Goldway Peak is off to our right and I went up the creek a ways. There is lots of moose sign here and I could have got a grouse today but the gun [.22] wouldn't fire. I finally got one squirrel for Snuffy to eat. The dogs are doing fine but are getting thin."

On May 7th the lads camped on what they named Fool Hen Creek,

Hap along a northern creek, 1947.

because they pigged out on four of them. They were in better game country now that they had left the river and were headed by compass to Johanson Creek. Hap noted, "Snuffy took off after a rabbit, pack and all. He came back, though. We are still about seven miles from Johanson and God knows we are tired of it now. The packs seem to get heavier every day."

By the next evening the lads were back on the Asitka River again heading for the lake. They had found the going too tough over the mountain. Once again they had an enjoyable meal after getting three more fool hens. "Hope to get some ducks or geese at the lake." Hap wrote, "Snow is sure going now and lots of bare ground. It sure is beautiful here by the river."

Hap's entry for May 9th read, "Got an early start but it started to rain so on with the damned snowshoes. We came a long way and then realized we are going down the wrong valley or canyon. We are not lost and if we get some meat everything will be okay. We only got one squirrel today for the dogs."

The following day the lads got an early start and headed up the mountain to find out where they had gone wrong. When they got up high, they spotted the lake and realized they had turned up the wrong creek. Then they began hearing strange sounds that turned out to be a flock of ptarmigan up near timberline. They managed to bag seven of them, and later in the day also bagged four blue grouse and a squirrel. "What a feast." Wrote Hap, "Our blues have gone."

For the next two days the lads checked for gold and hunted for grouse, always hoping that they would find a moose. They found that they couldn't pan, though, because of too much snow. They also found many blazes that were chopped out of the trees, probably put there by trappers and prospectors.

May 13th started out in a surprising way when they ran into a porcupine. Hap noted, "I shot the thing and as soon as it hit the ground, Sandy grabbed it. It's a good thing we had the pliers with us because he sure got a face full of quills. We got two grouse and Roy has the stew on; he's the cook today. We made about eight or nine miles today up and down hills over tough going. We sure gave her hell. Saw fresh bear sign, too. Then we found a shack, with a sign that read 'Jewel of the North' and it has a stove."

May 14th –"Up at daylight and went hunting. Got one ptarmigan and three fool hens. It is hard on the feet; shoes wet all the time. We just finished the last of the porcupine. Our dog Bob was so hungry he started eating my snowshoes; Roy caught him just in time."

May 15th –"What a day. We got up early to go hunting. We got three squirrels and seven fool hens. Then the dog ran into a porcupine and was fool enough to attack it. It was so full of quills that we had to shoot it. The best dog of them all, Old Sandy, has gone west where all good dogs go. We will feed him to the other dogs. We found a fish net and put it in the creek but we haven't had any luck. There are lots of bear and moose tracks around so hope we get one tomorrow."

Now that the young lads had a cabin to stay in things started looking up. They bathed, cleaned and washed everything in sight. The next project was obtaining food, so the boys went hunting. Roy trailed what he thought was a bear for several miles and when he got a look at it, it turned into a big wolf. He tried to shoot it but the gun misfired. He did all right, though, because he got back to the cabin with two blue grouse and four fool hens.

On the morning of the 17th Roy went hunting and cut a moose track on the fresh snow, then followed it for miles. He didn't have any luck with the moose, but he did manage to get two fool hens and a ptarmigan. When he got back to the cabin he just flopped down exhausted.

May 18th was Hap's turn to hunt. He wrote, "I took some lunch and climbed up the east end of Asitka Mountain hoping to find goat but didn't find anything. Then I crossed to the sunny side and got six fool hens. It is impossible to sneak up on a moose because we make too much noise in the snow. Oh! For a loaf of bread."

Over the next two days the lads hunted in earnest but only managed to bag three squirrels and ten fool hens. They were determined not to head for home without their pokes of gold, but by this time it had become obvious to them that they were losing their strength. The dogs were also growing weaker, having had to exist on a few squirrels and grouse remains.

At a loss for a solution to their problems, the lads packed up and decided to head for Johanson Lake in the hope of finding big game. On the evening of the 21st Hap wrote, "God! We both hated to hit the trail; the dogs whined too, but we didn't go very far before we got two ptarmigans. A couple miles later we hit fresh moose tracks and the dogs were off like bolt lightning, packs and all. They both got caught up in the brush so we had to go and release them. Then they were off again, as they were hungry too. The moose circled and got in the creek so the dogs couldn't get her. When I caught up she was heading downstream. I fired three shots and put her down, and when I got to her I could see that the wolves had played hell with her. She had lots of scars. A young cow with no fat."

During the excitement in the water, Hap had lost a snowshoe that floated away, so the next day Roy took his snowshoes and the dogs and packed in half the meat. In the afternoon Hap took the same snowshoes and brought in the other half with the dogs packing 50 pounds each.

The next day, May 23rd, was spent tearing an old cache apart and using the material to build a smoke house. The flies were up and about so the lads took no chances on losing the meat. After a hard day's work all the meat was cut up and hanging in the smoker. The big hope now was for a bear to come by and supply them with some much-needed fat, which they really missed. Without it they had been forced to eat a steady diet of boiled meat.

On May 24th Hap noted, "We had our first feed of smoked moose meat for breakfast and it sure is a hell of a change from boiled meat. We had it for dinner and supper too. Roy has lost at least 20 pounds and he looks a changed man since we left town. I just finished mending my pants by cutting up and using a towel for patches."

The long hot days of late May finally arrived and the snow dropped six inches on the 25th. The lads were sunbathing, having taken off their underwear for the first time. They used some large bandages as bathing suits and took some pictures.

Travel was restricted because Johanson Creek had risen considerably, but the morning hunt produced two fool hens, one with three eggs and the other with one egg. A great treat for the lads.

The next day produced another two fool hens, one with three eggs.

Hap sunbathing near Johanson Lake, 1947.

Hap wrote, "I had the hen and she was so fat that I was able to fry most of it. It was the best treat I've had since I got here. The moose meat that was smoked in big chunks is so good. We are eating at least 15 pounds a day. We never get full on it and I can't understand it. It is affecting us differently, Roy has the runs and I'm constipated."

Hap's message on the 27th stated, "Went out without snowshoes for the first time since we left Hazelton. Got a fool hen and a porcupine. It was good but Roy and I are getting awful weak. We really miss fat and vegetables. We are really sad because the flies got to our meat. All that smoking didn't stop them. We only have about 35 pounds left

33

so we are going to stay home and rest for a few days and then hit for the lake again. Roy is quite homesick for family and I don't feel too good either."

"It's sure tough when you're always hungry." Hap stated on the 28th day of May. "We got up late, ate moose meat and then went to get a sack of meat out of the creek. We cut it up in slices and put it out to dry. Searched for greens but not much so we tried eating grass but it was too dry. Should be more greens in a few days."

May 29th dawned sunny with a nice breeze. They packed up all their supplies and were ready to hit the trail when they heard an airplane. They rushed out the cabin door but it was out of sight. Hap wrote, "It made us feel as if there is someone else on this earth besides us. We both have pains in our stomachs when we take a deep breath. We have enough meat for one more day so if we don't find game we'll have to kill another dog."

"At Johanson Lake." Hap wrote. "What a day! We traveled around sloughs, hills and rocky country only to get here and find it as barren as the baldheaded prairies. Roy got a hen and I got a groundhog, the first animal I've seen with any fat on it. I guess we didn't cook it long enough because it tasted strong. I lit a fire and it got away and ran for half a mile, but it will stop when it hits the snowline. We were hoping to find ducks and geese but the ice is still on the lake. We found some berries from last year and we are eating them like mad."

The month of May ended in an unusual way for the two adventurers. Hap noted, "I couldn't sleep so I was looking at the mountain and was sure I saw something moving on top. I got Roy to look and he said it was goats. I crossed the lake and climbed to the peak of the mountain but I missed them. On the way back I found them but it was kind of dark to shoot. I fired about 20 rounds and saw one of them roll down the mountain. I brought it down and Roy had tea waiting for me."

The following day Hap wrote, "Roy sure had some tough luck. The fire burnt around and got into his pack, burnt most of his personal things such as his towel, camera and pictures. It even got his pants and coat. The shells were in his pants but they didn't explode. I didn't know what to say to comfort him."

Hap's diary entry for June 2nd was grim, "What a night. It blew and snowed three inches. What a damned country, our socks and boots and everything froze hard. We found some good-looking greens [possibly Indian hellebore] and Roy suggested I try some and then we could make stew if they are okay. I ate one and in one minute I knew I was poisoned. Roy made me drink some salt water and I managed to get most of it back up. I felt better so I ate some grouse, then I got sick again and really weak. It lasted that way all night."

"So many heartaches; too numerous to mention." So continued Hap's diary on June 3rd. "We have finally come to our senses and realized we are here in the gold belt and we are too weak to do anything about it. We are losing our strength more each day. We have decided to try to make it to Bear Lake about 60 miles from here. We hope the snow is gone enough and that we have the strength to make it there. We just can't gather any strength from this lean meat and there is no chance of a change in grub here. Our goat meat is not good to eat, although the dogs are doing all right on it."

June 4th – "We went hunting, got one grouse and a whistler [ground squirrel] and ate them. Then we tried to make it to the next cabin. We got about three miles when a plane flew over and cut its engine. We figured it would land on the lake so we walked back for nothing because it was not there. We came back to the spot we had been at when the plane came and made a stew. We got wet three times and Roy is sitting by the fire in his underwear. We got our dried meat all wet and lost the little axe when it slipped out of the dog's pack."

June 5th – "We are camped in a creek off Dortatelle Mountain; made about 20 miles today. We have thrown away our underwear and everything except our sleeping bags, which are wet. Got four grouse. Roy is taking samples off outcroppings to assay later. Our spirits are okay."

June 6th – "We went good for a ways and then came onto a grave 'Peter Himadan, August 7, 1939' is what the sign read [Peter was Simon Gunanoot's brother-in-law who was hunted by the police for 14 years]. We crossed the Quenada Creek and then had to climb over a mountain through three feet of snow. We got one grouse with three eggs and put them in the dog's saddlebags but he lost them in the swim. Hope to make Bear Lake tomorrow."

June 7th – "Don't know where we are for sure but think we're on Quenada Creek. We hit a cabin and we were sure lucky. There is a food cache here and we had a meal fit for a king. Got a grouse and a whistler today. We had to cross the creek twice and it sure is high from all the melting snow. I don't feel good and Roy looks tough, too.

It doesn't help not knowing where we are."

June 8th – "Roy and I are sure fools. We were so starved last night that we ate too many beans and then almost died from gas and dysentery. We found out that we are on Quenada Creek and we headed for the next cabin six miles away with only more beans for food. It took us all day to make it, and then I made the luckiest shot of my life. Four geese flew up about 200 yards from us and I got one of them. There is a meat grinder in this cabin so we pulled off the fat and made hamburgers out of the legs and breast. This is the first fat we have had for one month. Hope it will give us strength for the trail tomorrow."

June 9th – "If we weren't in snow up to our ass, we were in mud, or else we were looking for the trail. Roy got a porky and I got a groundhog so we are still eating. I've never missed as many shots as I did today. We walked 10 hours and made about 12 miles. Our stew pot holds three gallons and we ate it all up in one meal. We are both dreaming of a big feed of hotcakes at Bear Lake."

June 10th – "The longest hike I've ever put in but we made it. I never was so glad to get out of the mountains as I was tonight. We plowed through snow all day, lots of it, and I just can't put it in writing. We've hit an Indian cabin and they have fresh fish . . . What a feed, and we talked long into the night. The boys here are really kind and do everything they can to help us. I can't see why these Indians are treated so bad."

June 11th – "What a day. We sure are glad to be out of the mountains; the Indians can't believe we did it this time of year. I showed them the plant I had eaten and they said it would kill a horse in no time. We broke into the store and took lots of grub, flour, rice, raisins and everything but still no butter or lard, which we crave so much. I wrote out a cheque for the supplies. We got an old Indian to take us to the end of the lake, about 15 miles, and we talked all the way. He's all buggered up from something, but I've got his name and I'm going to send him up some rum when I get out."

June 13th – "Our digestive systems are off because of all this good food again. We have been eating bannock, rice and fish soup all day and we're still hungry all the time. The Indians told us that the Sustut Canyon is impossible to go through, but we did it."

June 14th – "Flies are so bad I can hardly write. We have taken a beating on the trail today. Our legs are all cramped up from the long hike over the mountain by Bear Lake. We only made about six miles today because our legs cramped up all the time. We didn't even see a grouse today and we were in good game country with lots of lakes and a good trail. The hunger pains are wearing down now."

June 15th – "We had a fair day on the trail; made about 15 miles. Had some good luck when we came to a cabin and found some mineral oil and some olive oil. We made some hotcakes and they sure hit the spot. We had to cross one big creek [Lion Creek, perhaps] today and we almost lost our last dog. I tried to hold on to him but the water was so deep and swift that he upset me. We nearly both went down in the current. We're in good spirits now and hope to make it to Takla Lake tomorrow."

June 16th – "Beautiful country and lots of moose, too. I don't know why but my toenails are falling off. My feet are killing me, especially the one I spilled hot tea on. We made 25 miles today and still have that much to do tomorrow. There is a lot of bear sign but we haven't ran into any. The dog is all in, he doesn't want to move."

June17th – "We made 10 miles through the bush, swamps and flies. We stopped to make cocoa and ran into some Indians that were fishing. They had a boat so they took us 10 miles down the lake to the Hudson's Bay store and took us into their fully modern home. I could hardly believe it: bacon and eggs; peaches and cream; cookies and chocolates; ketchup, coffee and bread. What a meal, and a bunkhouse to sleep in. We really had lots of things to talk about."

From Takla Lake our heroes caught a ride to Fort St. James by scow, where they learned that it had been pilot Pat Carey who had flown over them at Johanson Lake. In fact, he had landed, forced down by bad weather. They didn't see the airplane because it was a silver colour and blended in with the lake. They also met bush pilot Russ Baker, and were surprised at the great interest everyone took in their adventures.

Both men were full of praise for all the help and understanding they received toward the conclusion of their journey. They tried to hire on at some of the mines in the area but found that they were at least a week too late as the outfits already had their crews. One of the highlights of their days in Fort St. James was meeting and staying with the Bob Hoy family, who were celebrating their parents' 50th anniversary at the time. Hap noted, "Bob Hoy has a lovely sister." More than just a little impressed with the people around Fort St. James, Hap set about getting many autographs, among them noted

Hap, 1947.

bush pilots Russel Baker and Capt. Pat Carey. Also included in the list are several members of the Hoy Family, famous freighters along the chain of lakes for many years.

As for Hap and Roy, their adventure was over, so after waiting several days for money to arrive from Vancouver, the young adventurers were finally on their way home.

When we take a critical look back at the trying journey made by these two young men it becomes apparent that they were exceptionally lucky to survive. The fact that Hap's toenails started coming off toward the end of the trip served notice that their bodies were desperately short of vitamin C (ascorbic acid). In short, they were flirting with scurvy. In adults, scurvy remains latent for three to six months after vitamin C intake drops below 10 mg/day. But other factors come into play: such as long hours of plodding through deep snow, which accelerates the metabolism. Heat or cold stress, such as the lads endured wading the icy streams day after day, increases urinary excretion. Also, cooking can destroy vitamin C and cooked food is mostly what they ate.

This vitamin C deficiency was so unnecessary as the needles on the trees all around them were loaded with ascorbic acid; all they had to do was make tea with them. But the lads were unaware of this fact. Had their journey lasted for several more months, Hap and Roy may have suffered the fate of many early-day forest wanderers who died from scurvy.

After his return from the wilderness Hap expressed his feelings of the venture with the following poem:

Here is solitude and yet
A world of beauty, a land we can't forget.
Where nature beckons within our souls we bless
A spot of freedom in God's loneliness.

CHAPTER TWO
CLARA WARD

Clara Amanda Ward was born in Burnaby, BC on August 17th, 1926. One of 14 children out of whom only ten survived. Her family was on relief throughout her childhood, but that didn't mean they were housebound. Her father was a musician who wrote his own music, and he taught all the children to play music as well.

The book *Green Branches and Fallen Leaves* is the story of Shawnigan Lake. Among its pages is the following item:

"In 1928 there came to Shawnigan Mr. and Mrs. Tom Ward with their little family of three. By the time twelve years had elapsed their family numbered ten and they had achieved, not a baseball team, but a full-fledged family orchestra. In 1932 the S.L.A.A. had sponsored an amateur night at which the first prize was won by the Ward Instrumentalists, a family then of four eager little children, playing on instruments almost bigger than themselves and led by their musical father. From this encouraging start, the little orchestra gradually increased to eight pieces, nine counting the father. In 1940 a benefactor hailing from Courtenay, and preferring to be known only to the press of that time as 'H.L.', arranged a tour for the little orchestra

Clara's parents, Tom and Elizabeth, 1945.

through Canada and the United States. At that time the players ages and instruments were as follows: Marjorie, 17, E-flat bass; James, 15, second cornet; Clara, 13, slide trombone; Doris, 12, French horn; Walter, 12, trap-drummer; Lawrence, 8, cymbal; Lillian, 6, conductor; Dennis, 4, triangle; and Mr. Ward, solo cornet."

"Mr. Ward received his musical training at Kneller Hall, London, England and was with the original Dumbells in France. Mrs. Ward was also musical, playing piano. The children got their instruments by earning them, largely through theatre appearances in Duncan. The Wards' original instruments included an organ, guitar-zither, a cornet and a French horn. Besides their Duncan performances, they played over the air in Victoria and Vancouver and gave programs all over the Island. The Ward family did not return to Shawnigan after their tour but settled on the mainland where it is hoped that they were able to continue their promising careers."

During the summer of 1939 the family set off on a trip across Canada. In many cities along the way they stopped and played on street corners. By this means they were able to feed themselves and pay the vehicle costs as well.

Ward Family Band after Canadian Tour, 1940.

For eight years Clara worked for Safeway in Vancouver, and it was while so employed that she had a rather interesting day. This event took place because it was Clara's turn to watch from a peephole for shoplifters, and while so doing, she hit pay dirt. A well-known minister's wife entered the store and while Clara watched in amazement, began stuffing a great supply of goods up into her bloomers. Clara reported the theft to her superior but he refused to believe it. Slightly

Clara Ward, February, 1947.

befuddled, her boss followed the woman out to her car and questioned her about the theft. While she was busy denying it, a jar of pickles rolled out on the ground. The woman was brought back into the store where she was detained while the manager phoned the main store requesting their advise on how to deal with the situation. At last someone came from the main store and after a long discussion, allowed the woman to leave without prosecution. Her only penalty was that she was banned from that store.

When asked how she met her future husband, Hap Bowden, Clara replied, "At a house party." Apparently Hap got another woman at the party to get Clara's address and once he got back to his logging camp, he started corresponding with her. Sneaky devils, us men, aren't we?

Hap defends himself by saying, "It was love at first sight."

When I asked Clara if Hap really put the rush on her, she replied, "He didn't dance with any other woman all evening."

Clara and Hap met in 1948 and were married in 1949, while Clara was employed at Safeway. During this time Hap was working long hours driving truck in the Vancouver area. They saved their money as best they could and planned to start a taxi business, but this venture fell through at the last minute. Clara recalls trading her roller skates straight across for a sewing machine and this turned out to be one of the best investments she ever made, because throughout the years she put it to good use. She became an expert seamstress who made quality coats, sweaters, mitts, curtains, and just about everything else one can imagine.

Hap and Clara's wedding. It was love at first sight, 1949.

In 1951 they purchased a new car and headed north in search of a new life. A couple business ventures were discussed and thrown aside as the new Bowden family attempted to sink their teeth into a life of adventure. Little could they imagine what an unbelievable amount of adventure was in store for them.

In April, Clara and Hap arrived in Quesnel where they embarked on a new life. Hap got a job in a mill and they moved into the Red Bluff Motel where they paid $45 a month rent. Just a short time later the motel owner told them that the tourist season was at hand and that the rent would jump to $65 a month. This was more than the Bowden family wanted to pay so they went to work on a different project. They purchased two and a half acres of land and in two days built a tiny cabin eight by eight feet square. When they put a bed, a stove and a table inside their new home there was barely room to stand. Hap claims that this was the only place he has ever lived where he was able to light the fire without getting out of bed.

Clara in window of cabin that was built in two days.

Clara still shakes her head as she recalls a storm that hit just a short time after they moved into their new mansion. They were the largest hailstones she has ever seen, and it didn't take long for them to beat their way through the tarpaper on the roof. They had used green lumber on the roof and covered it with tarpaper, so as the boards dried they left gaps, with only the tarpaper between the weather and the inner cabin. As Clara stood in the doorway holding their dog in her arms, the hail broke through and covered everything in the cabin

The second cabin was better.

including their bed. I asked Hap if she was crying when he got home from work and he replied, "No! She was too tough for that."

The Bowdens didn't stay very long in their two-day cabin. They went to work in their spare time and quickly constructed a cozy little cabin with an addition. Hap could no longer light the fire without getting out of bed.

Hap did not enjoy town life; he longed for a free type of life where he could be his own person, and with hard work and vision, get ahead in the world. With Clara's full support he began searching for an alternative life style.

During the summer of 1952 they purchased some acreage on lot 8328 about 25 miles southeast of Quesnel. The original owner, a man named Holland, had passed away and was buried on his property. Then the land was put up for sale and the next owner, Netterstrom, sold it to Clara and Hap. This was exactly what the Bowdens had been looking for so they leapt at the chance. It was located in a little valley along Beaver Creek and had a portion of a lake and its own meadows. As well, being that he was a war veteran, Hap was given another 160 acres of Crown Grant land adjacent to his new property. All told, there was some excellent timber on this property and a creek with willow flats that produced some fine beaver pelts. This area was

47

Clara with Rocky and chickens in the crates.

well off the beaten track and was accessible only by a trail that wandered through the forest for five miles. This meant all their possessions had to be carried through the forest on horseback.

Clara remembers the evening she was leading one of the horses through the forest toward the farm when trouble overtook her. The horse was carrying two boxes on its back and each box contained several chickens that were being transported to their new home. Just as they approached the farm, they had to descend a steep hill and Clara was afraid to lead the horse for fear it would fall on her. Left with no alternative she set the horse free to descend as it pleased. Part way down the hill the horse tried to pass between two trees that grew close together. There wasn't enough room, though, so both boxes were torn apart and chickens were seen running in all directions.

It was getting dark by that time, so Clara just went on to the farm. The next morning she found that all the chickens had made it to the farm and each one had laid an egg during the night. Clara joked that they considered banging the chickens against a tree each evening just to see if the trend would continue.

Clara and Hap were getting set up in their new life and a giant step was taken when they purchased a Jersey milk cow for $75. This provided them with milk, butter and that most delicious of desserts – homemade ice cream.

Clara with Rosie's first calf May, 1955.

The cow had been bred and soon produced a calf, so along with their horses they were on the way to independence. This beautiful little valley with its stream, lake and solitude would turn out to be their home for many years to follow.

CHAPTER THREE
THE EARLY YEARS

L ife was a constant challenge and adventure on their new farm that was soon named the Diamond B Bar Ranch. Clara's diary is replete with entries detailing the endless chores and work that faced them. There are many entries that show how they lived off the land and the appreciation they felt for this bounty. One entry describes Hap bringing home a catch of fish and just how delicious they tasted. Grouse were taken from the willow thickets and again added to the larder of this family that knew hard times during their first years in the forest.

During the summer of 1952 Clara and Hap proceeded to build a log house but because of a shortage of funds it was not completed. By 1955 they noticed that rot had started in the corners so they tore it down and cut the logs into lumber with which they later built a big barn.

The house built in 1952 and torn down in 1955.

In March 1954 Hap felt ambitious so he fell a cottonwood tree and set about building a dugout canoe. This was a time-consuming job but the end result was worth it. At the completion of the job they celebrated by having the greatest treat the woods can ever offer–homemade ice cream. Only people who have tasted ice cream made from real cream can possibly know just how delicious it is, especially in a wilderness setting.

As soon as the nearby lake was free of ice, Hap and a friend took the dugout canoe for a trial run. In her diary entry Clara noted, "They got dunked." When I questioned Hap about it he admitted that it was a bit top heavy and that he solved the problem by putting some sand in the bottom of the canoe and adding a keel for stability.

Their next project was to start building a cabin for the hunters they would soon be guiding. This was a project where Clara's many talents really came to the fore. In one day she packed four sacks of moss from the forest that she used

Clara, Hap and the boys in Hap's dugout canoe.

to chink between the logs of the cabin. As well as having an endless amount of housework that was always waiting for her, Clara made many things for the cabin that saved them a great deal of money: such as curtains for the windows that she made out of flour sacks, or towels made from salt bags. Nothing was wasted. Even worn-out socks were remade into mitts. One of the fine coats she made is still in the Bowden household. This coat is the equal of any coat made anywhere. It was made from a Hudson's Bay blanket that cost $172. It is a bit heavy, but would keep a person warm in almost any weather.

Money was often in short supply during the early years on the ranch. For that reason Hap went to work for Malimac Mills during the winter months. At the same time Clara was hired as cook. Back at the ranch the horses were well supplied with feed because they had access to a large haystack. But then tragedy struck. Clara's brother-in-law visited the ranch and unwittingly closed the pasture gate, thereby

53

Hap and Joe Guibault splitting shakes.

denying the horses' access to the stack. When Hap and Clara returned to the farm they were staggered to find four of their horses had starved to death. This was a near unbearable loss and a huge setback to their guide-outfitting plans.

By the spring of 1954, a great many projects were under way. The hunter's cabin had just been finished but there were endless chores still facing them. There were fences to build, a chicken house to build, and a garden to plant. Clara had her hands full, what with milking the cow, cleaning house, and the never-ending job of baking bread, so tasty fresh from the oven. One entry in her diary noted that along with all her other jobs she had made apple and rhubarb pies and then made root beer, a welcome treat on a hot summer day. Another entry noted that Hap had caught a large beaver and was very pleased. The money that came in from furs was badly needed for the many expenses associated with their new life on Bowden Ranch.

Hap spent many an hour clearing land and pulling stumps with his three horses. From morning till night smoke rose above the ranch as brush fires were kept burning. Certainly the Bowdens had no time for

Walter Evans and Hap pulling stumps.

boredom. When there were spare moments the Bowdens put them to good use by fishing for trout at Beaver Falls about a half-mile distant from the ranch. Hap also found a bit of time to go prospecting, a love that was to fill a large portion of their future years.

On one of his many visits to the ranch, Hap's father came to help with their many projects. Clara took note of his ability to remember songs and poems. Obviously touched, she recited his favorite poem for me:

"When the golden sun is setting and the earth no more you trod
May your name in gold be written in the autograph of God."

At the age of 80, Hap's father still had an outstanding memory. They watched in amazement as he sat at their table and wrote out about eighty songs from memory.

One of Hap's favorite stories concerned two pioneer friends that worked together in the long ago. On a trip to the city one of the men purchased a pocket watch and then came home and proceeded to flaunt it in front of his partner. After eyeing the watch for a while the friend asked, "What time is it?"

The watch owner proudly held it up for his friend to see and then, being unable to tell time, answered, "See, that's what time it is right there!"

Hap's mother and father, Florence and Albert.

His friend, who was also unable to tell time, looked at it for a minute and then exclaimed, "I'll be damned; it is too."

Life wasn't all fun and games, though, as Hap found out on June 23. He went prospecting with a friend and was traveling along on horseback when his horse lost its footing and landed upside down with Hap beneath it. The saddle horn drove into Hap's leg while the saddle landed on his other leg. Though injured, Hap continued working on the ranch until the pain in his leg became unbearable. Finally, at the insistence of Clara, he went into Quesnel and had Dr. Thompkins lance the injury, which was terribly swollen. Clara noted that Hap stayed in bed for a few days even though he had a million chores waiting for him.

Sometimes the smallest thing seemed so important, such as the diary entry that they had eaten wild strawberries for the first time. Another time Clara noted that she had made a nest for a setting hen and then found another hen setting on 11 eggs out near the corral.

July was perhaps the busiest month of the year, what with cutting, turning, raking and then putting up hay. During this time there were cows to milk, butter to make and an endless amount of work in the garden. Repairing and making new fences was a summer-long project.

Each step they took added to the overall potential of the ranch, and a big step was taken in June when they purchased a crawler tractor. They felt that this machine was a must if their dream of logging and ranching was to be a success. It didn't turn out that way, though, because the tractor was totally lacking in power. Hap jokes that it was the best tractor ever made for pushing water downhill.

Soon they also bought a power saw and a jeep. Things were definitely looking up on the Diamond B Bar Ranch. Perhaps it was possible that their wilderness dreams, getting ahead by hard work and an aggressive nature, could come true.

With a power saw in his hands Hap set to falling timber in a big way. On June 13th Clara noted that Hap had worked 10 hours, and that she had made a batch of beer. Sometimes they would book off on a Sunday for a much-needed rest. This would often include a picnic at Beaver Falls while fishing for trout, or perhaps a fishing trip by canoe along the nearby lake. The day would sometimes be capped by a bowl of wild strawberries or strawberry shortcake.

Beaver Falls – a favourite fishing spot.

Bath night was a special occasion as the water had to be carried and then heated on the stove. In at least one case Hap, obviously exhausted from a tiring day's work, took a short cut and bathed in the creek shortly before midnight.

On July 24th, 1954, Clara went to Quesnel and then on to Vancouver where she stayed with her family while awaiting her first-born. Meanwhile, Hap had been busy guiding back in the mountains. This meant he was elected cook. One evening after the hunters had finished eating the main course, Hap opened a jar of rhubarb fruit and placed it on the table. The boys went for it, and no sooner had they tasted it, then they all politely stopped eating. Puzzled, Hap took a spoonful and swallowed it, then jumped out of his chair. It didn't take long for him to realize that Clara had canned the rhubarb without sugar. Apparently they were a good bunch of boys because Hap managed to get out of camp alive.

Their firstborn, Brad, came into this world on October 13th and Hap went to Vancouver to be with them. Between his visits to the hospital, Hap found time to appear on Ted Peck's TV Show, *Tight Lines, Straight Shooting*. His reason for being on the show was to display a huge set of mule deer antlers. Hap still retains the cheque stub #109014 in the amount of $15 that he received from the CBC for appearing on the show. This was just one of an endless number of interviews he had with the media throughout the years. Clara informed me that the story of the big deer was rather unusual in that several of Hap's friends had already got their deer and they were teasing him about not getting one. Hap joked that he was just waiting for a giant to come along and darned if it didn't.

One of Clara's memories concerns her trip back to Quesnel from Vancouver with her newborn son, Brad. It was just a few days before Christmas 1954,

Hap's big deer made the record book.

when they caught a ride up the Likely Highway to Beavermouth, where they expected to meet Hap. He was supposed to be there with their team of horses to bring them the last five miles to their ranch. A heavy snowfall had plugged the road to the point where the horses could not get through, so in desperation Hap had attempted to open the road with a tractor. As luck would have it, the tractor had broken down and so Clara and Brad were stranded. Two elderly bachelor Swedes, who were mining in the area, lived at Beavermouth at the time and they generously offered to share their cabin. Clara was to use the room of Victor Ericson, while he shared the other room with Ole Olson, with the addition of a cot.

The second day at their place Clara was forced to wash diapers. Just as she finished and hung them up to dry above the stove, they noticed a neighboring trapper coming for a visit. The two Swedes decided to play a joke on their visitor so they asked Clara to hide in the other room. When Mr. Pritchard entered he quickly freaked out when he noticed the many diapers hanging from the line. Before the trapper's imagination had time to run away with him, the baby started crying and the joke was over.

After two days with the miners, the repairs were made to the tractor, the road was plowed, and at last Clara and Brad got to their ranch at Bowden Creek.

Before I leave these two bachelor miners, I must relate the following story. Hap asked Ole what they did for entertainment during the long winter nights and he answered, "Sometimes we read a little bit in the evenings."

Then Victor added, "Yaw, and sometimes we read a little bit in the daytime too." Doesn't sound like a very exciting life, does it?

On August 25th Clara noted that she has made moccasins and pajama bottoms for Brad, weeded the garden, roasted half a leg of venison and cut Hap's hair as well. A week later they went to the Coast to visit Hap's dad and Clara's family. On their return she noted that she had purchased 54 yards of flannelette @ 25 cents a yard. This was used to make diapers, but Clara also pointed out that she made a dress from it and it cost a total of 29 cents for the flannelette.

Hunting season came and went with more hunters taking home a winter's meat supply. One hunter, Tony Batty, was overjoyed when he took home a record moose.

Winter 1954/55 was a new experience for Clara now that she had a baby in the house. For Hap, there was always an endless cycle of chores, such as falling trees for the second cabin they were going to build. These cabins were a must because the Bowdens were into guiding with the hope of expanding their business each year, as if they didn't have enough on their plate already.

April found them working from dawn till dusk, clearing and burning brush to enlarge the hayfields. For much hay would be needed to winter the cattle and horses that were a part of their dreams. As well, there was a lot of work to be done on the house and miles of fences to build.

Tony Batty displays his moose antlers with 54-inch spread.

Throughout the months of May and June Hap and Clara finished their third cabin for hunters. In all, they ended up with a total of 18 cabins. Hap was also busy falling trees, in some cases putting in over 10 hours. As well as all her household chores, Clara found time to milk cows, plant and weed garden, and by far the most important of all – make beer.

July 2nd, 1955 rated mentioning in Clara's diary because it was picnic day. The family went to Beaver Falls where Hap caught the first rainbow trout of the year. Then they were off to the lake for some swimming and canoeing. When they returned to the ranch they had strawberries and fresh cream waiting for them, and the following day, strawberry shortcake. In spite of their endless chores, the family always made sure there was time for pleasure and enjoyment. Proof that they did a bit of partying was supplied when Clara noted, "Hap and Cliff went to town and got into some beer; Hap is pretty sick today."

Finally their dreams started to come true, and this became apparent on October 27th when Clara noted, "Hunters left this morning with two moose. We got $200 from them."

This sum may seem insignificant today, but at that time it was equal to several months' take-home pay. And this was just a start, because Hap and Clara would turn out to be first class guides with clientele that proved they were satisfied by returning year after year.

Progress was steady at the ranch and the arrival of a washing machine was greeted by Clara with this note, "Did my first washing of diapers with the machine today; what a difference."

At this same time Hap hired a couple men and started up a sawmill. A few days later the Bowdens put their first deposit in the bank.

Christmas was a pleasant surprise for Hap, because when he opened his present he found a beautiful knitted sweater from Clara. Across the front of it was a horse standing by a fence with the Diamond Bar B brand on it.

Throughout the winter months, the men worked the sawmill and Clara found herself cooking for as many as nine people. This wasn't enough to keep her hands busy so she began knitting and selling sweaters. Among her notes was one dated March 11th, which read, "We bought a mare for $25."

Step by step their ranch was becoming a reality.

Another winter of hard work passed by with more and more assets being accumulated, such as the arch for the cat that facilitated moving timber from the forest. One entry read, "We tried to go to town today but the road was washed out. Hap fell a tree across the road so no one would drive into the washout. Dave had his car on the other side of the washout, so we got to town anyway."

Crossing a washout with the Landrover.

These washouts were a regular occurrence, with Spring Creek washing out 13 years in a row.

Clara told me about one of their trips out from the ranch to where they left their vehicle near Beavermouth. The road was so muddy that they were forced to follow the creek and carry Brad in their arms for over five miles (eight kilometers). In one of the places where they had to cross the creek, they were forced to jump. Clara made it, but the shopping bag she carried came apart and all her letters, which were to be mailed, landed in the creek. After a brief chase the letters were recovered, but they all had to be rewritten because they were sopping wet.

It becomes apparent when reading the diary that the people in that general area continually assisted each other. For instance, the following day Hap had his Cat out filling the washout and then went on to clear land for Dave Bow.

There were times of frustration, though, such as the day in May when the Cat broke down. Hap had to go to Quesnel and order the part. Since it was not available in Canada, they had to wait and lost two weeks work before it arrived.

May 18th, 1956 was a memorable day for the Bowden family for that was the day that Albert "Ab" Bowden entered the world. Always brief, Clara wrote, "Hap brought me a dozen roses." A couple days later she added, "I had to come home early because Brad's nose is out of joint. Anytime I give Ab a bottle I have to give him one, too."

An entry for June 2nd read. "Hap and a friend went to town and got a bottle, then came home sick. I gave them heck."

Since the next writing indicates that the friend packed up and moved to Vancouver the following day, I was forced to ask Hap, "Is it true that she gave you guys heck?"

"I think the word 'hell' would be a more accurate description." He replied.

Several times throughout that time period Clara mentioned that Brad loved it outdoors and absolutely hated to come into the house. Perhaps it should be no surprise that he became a big game guide in later years.

Purchases were coming in droves by this time. On June 7th they bought a horse named Red. The next day they purchased a new tractor with accessories. A week later they started construction of an addition to the house, so badly needed now that they had steady boarders. Clara noted, "Hap got out logs for an A frame. I lifted him and the A frame up with the tractor so he could put a block and tackle on it." The foregoing shows that Clara was Hap's right arm, capable of doing any job on the place. Casually thrown into the entry was the mention that they had gone to Beavermouth with the team and buckboard. Not as simple as it may appear, because sometimes the road was just a sea of mud.

By the time July rolled around they were haying and hauling in logs for an addition to the house. Always innovative, they placed a car seat on the back of their tractor and used it to go to where their vehicle was parked at Beavermouth.

An August entry notes that Hap arrived home with some fish and a deer. Once again it was time for Clara to get out the canner and put away preserves for winter. She also mentioned that they corned some of the venison.

Some excitement was stirred in the valley on August 12th when Hap's helpers, Herb and George, got lost in the forest. They finally found their way home, arriving after midnight.

By the 14th of August a major milestone was accomplished. At a cost of $6000, which really put a drag on the Bowdens' account, a road was completed into the ranch. The next day Clara wrote, "Hap had to pull the cars up the hill with the Cat." This was just the first of countless times that vehicles had to be towed out of the valley. The next day another first took place when a load of peeled logs was shipped out. The Bowdens had many ventures on the go and it seemed almost certain that some of them would succeed.

Sometimes there was a downside to opening up the road as it took just a short period of time for word to get around that there was good fishing to be had at Beaver Falls as well as at the lake. Soon there was a steady stream of vehicles coming to the ranch. In an effort to control the situation, a "private road" sign had to be erected. It didn't do much good, though, because many so-called friends were to take advantage of their hospitality and grace their kitchen table, as we shall see. On the bright side, a man named Gordon Spier used to plow their road with a grader, and the distance was so great that he had to spend a night at the ranch on each trip.

Proof that there was more than just work going on at the Bowden ranch was supplied on September 8th, 1956 when they took 27-dozen beer bottles to town. The refund amounted to 20 cents a dozen or the sum total of $5.40.

On September 23rd, Herb bagged a fat bull moose. This meant that Clara spent the next many days canning moose meat. Meanwhile, the men were building on the addition. When the doorway was cut into the addition, Clara noted, "The place sure seems big now."

Mixed in with all the other chores, Hap and Herb graveled the road up the hill in an effort to stop vehicles from getting stuck there. As well, they were building fence and getting firewood for the winter months.

October 8th was an important day at the Bowden Ranch, because two hunters arrived from Victoria. On the 9th they got a buck deer. On the 11th John got his moose. On the 12th Bill got his moose. On the 14th Bill and John went fishing. On the 16th Bill and John got another deer. And finally on the 17th the hunters left for Victoria with two moose and two deer. It is not hard to imagine hunters wanting to return after they had such great luck. Something else that warrants mentioning is that this game was usually hung high up on a 70-foot tripod. Hap says this kept the meat away from the flies, which stay closer to the ground.

Another undertaking was tackled on October 31st, when Hap and Herb began work on a large addition to the barn. More space was desperately needed for their cattle and the many horses necessary for guiding. Four days later some men were moved into the camp at the mill-site just above the ranch, where they began sawing lumber. The next day Clara proudly noted, "First load of lumber went out today. The three men working at the sawmill are boarding here."

Seventy-foot tripod for hanging deer above the flies.

Clara had to present herself to her dentist on November 5th where she had two teeth removed. The cost totaled $3.50. The next day hunters arrived on a one-day hunt and paid Hap $40 for the one day. The comparison of prices for the teeth and the hunt clearly show why

63

Hap and Clara wanted to get into guiding in a big way.

The next order of business was to put a roof on the sawmill and build shacks for the crew. This was accomplished and the crew moved in and started batching for themselves. Soon there were six families living at the mill-site.

Just how much they lived off the land was emphasized on November 9th when Clara wrote, "Hap got a deer and a moose; duck for dinner and moose liver for supper."

Now that there was a supply of sawdust at the mill, it followed that Clara should get a sawdust burner for the house. Once installed, this spared a great deal of time that had previously been spent on falling, hauling and splitting firewood. Step by step things were improving for the Bowdens.

All through the months leading up to Christmas, Hap worked hard falling and hauling trees to the sawmill. In between he even found time to bring home two deer. On December 6th Clara wrote, "It's minus 38 today, just hugging the stove." And again, "Hap and Herb went to town today. They slid in the ditch and had to get Eugene to drive them home. Then he tried to go out with the tractor to get the jeep but he couldn't climb the hill. Now he has been plowing the road with the Cat for 10 hours."

Clara got a terrible scare on December 16th. She thought Brad was up at the mill-site so she went up to get him. When she arrived she learned that he hadn't been there, so she rushed back to the house and broke down crying. Brad, who had been hiding, came out when he saw her tears. In her diary she wrote, "What a scare!"

On the brighter side of things there was always a constant sense of humour around the ranch. Hap's jokes were well known to all and I wouldn't doubt that this humour has added to their health and longevity. Perhaps a good place to start describing this humour concerns a trip Clara and Hap took to Barkerville. On their arrival Hap rented a gold pan for 50 cents and along with several other people, started panning for gold in a place that had been salted for that purpose. After shaking his pan around and feigning ignorance, Hap asked some of the other people what the colours were in his pan. The boss ran over to him, looked in his pan, and couldn't believe what he was seeing. Grudgingly, the boss panned it out and placed the ounce of gold in a couple vials for Hap to take home, but he was not a happy camper. He figured he had screwed up somehow and placed too much gold in the gravel. To this day Hap has never let on that it was his own gold.

If you ask Hap what method of birth control he used to limit his family to two children, his reply is a lesson in simplicity: he simply placed a rock in his shoe and it made him go limp.

Hap set me up on another of his jokes when he told me that he had never had a venereal disease in his life. When I asked the obvious question as to what he wore to protect himself, he answered, "A wedding ring, and it never let me down once in 53 years."

Determined to pursue the sex thing with Hap, I asked him if he ever used an aphrodisiac and he offered that he had tried it once. When I asked him to elaborate, he went on, "Years ago they used to say that oysters were an aphrodisiac but I know for sure that they aren't, because I ate 30 of them one weekend and only 17 worked."

When New Year's Eve rolled around and 1957 approached Hap and Clara felt a bit lonesome, so about 11:30 p.m. Hap walked up to the mill-site, woke everyone up and invited them down for a party. They all brought in the New Year together by dancing and, I suspect, consuming some white lightning. The reason I suspect that is because Clara noted in her diary the next day, "Had turkey dinner; Hap not so hot after last night." Two weeks later she noted, "I started some home brew."

Late January brought in some mean temperatures. Clara described the 26th to the 28th as between -10 and -50 degrees. The vehicles were stuck until the Public Works came to their rescue.

By spring time, Hap had given up on the sawmill he had rented from Patchetts and had moved in his own mill instead. On April 5th they cut 46 ties. On the 8th they cut 22 ties and 500 feet of lumber. Soon they were cutting 70 ties a shift.

During the month of May Hap was trapping beaver, cutting lumber for the addition to the house, as well as digging a basement and working at the mill. Soon 100 sacks of cement arrived for the basement.

The new mill was producing up to expectations with a record cut of 90 ties on June 6th. Clara was busy cooking for five men while tending her garden and doing household chores. As well, the game warden and two policemen showed up to fish at the falls. Extra company was a common occurrence at the Bowden table. The officers were a few days early, though, because if they had arrived five days later they would have caught Hap with a buck deer. If he had been caught, Hap probably would have echoed another old woodsman who said, "How are the game wardens supposed to know when I need meat?"

On June 17th and 18th they poured 35 sacks of concrete for the basement. On the 21st the first cheque arrived for the ties. On the 22nd they cut 90 ties. On the 23rd the front wall of the house was put up. On the 24th the back and right walls came up. On the 27th Hap and Herb were pouring concrete for a cistern when they discovered something was wrong with the cattle. The men rushed into town to find out and returned to treat the cattle for pink eye.

On July 2nd they were putting sheeting on the roof. Over the next two months they had finished the closets and partitions, built a chimney, hauled rocks and poured concrete for the fireplace. Hap helped the electrician with all the wiring and they began stuccoing the house. Next came the aluminum roofing, and during the free moments they were graveling the road, which was in terrible condition from a steady month of rain. Clara helped every way possible, even doing the milking to free up the men. During this time they tried their best to get in

Brad and Ab Bowden's faces reflect their feelings when told by their father that the pups had to go.

some hay, but because of the eternal rain, they had little luck.

A priceless event occurred late that summer when their dog had pups. The boys instantly fell in love with the cute little pups, so we can scarcely imagine their shock when Hap informed them that the pups had to go. The accompanying photo plainly shows their reactions to the news. The expressions on their faces could well read, "Over our dead bodies."

As they were unable to keep all the pups, Hap took them to Quesnel just as school was getting out for the day. He gave a pup to each of several boys and then told them to take them home and ask their mothers if they could keep them. Hap added that he would wait for a while in case they had to bring them back. After a long wait Hap was just getting ready to leave when one of the boys returned with a pup in his arms and shouted, "Get the hell out of here, I told Mom that you left already."

Hap took the hint and left.

The family was so busy during this period that they hired four ditch-diggers to assist at the ranch for two days. This cost them $221, a tidy sum of money in 1957, but it was worth it to have running

The ranch with two hunting cabins.

water in the house. The last job was to put in the plumbing and that completed, the family moved into their new home on September 19th. This was a momentous occasion by any standard, and Clara wrote, "I never realized we had so much stuff." To top off their enjoyment they managed to get in the last of the hay, which had lain on the fields for weeks.

And then there was the day that Hap almost got a surprise when he shot a buck deer. The next day the game warden dropped by to say that he had arrested four men the day before for shooting a moose before the season opened.

October was also memorable because Hap returned from town with a 1954 Willy's jeep, a stove for the cabin and a bouquet of flowers for Clara. With the hot water hooked up, Clara wrote, "I cleaned house today but I don't know if I'll ever get rid of the dust."

Since Hap's life is so full of humour, I must throw in a few of his many jokes, such as the fellow that met his friend on the trail and asked, "How's your wife, Jack?"

Back came the reply, "Oh, better than nothing I guess."

And then I must meet the balancing act of fairness by telling the one where the woman asked her friend, "Your husband doesn't say much, does he?"

"No," the other woman responded, "but that sure doesn't stop him from talking."

Another groaner from Hap was his admittance that he is steadily getting stronger with age. For proof he adds that he used to have to take the horse and buggy to town to haul $50 worth of groceries and that now he can carry $50 worth in one hand.

Getting back to guiding, game wasn't always readily available, as Hap found out that November. Clara tells how both the hunter and Hap returned saddle sore without any game. Four days later she noted, "The hunter left today with a moose and a deer." Clara also wrote, "We took a 300-pound steer to town and sold it. Got $35 for it."

Hap started off the 1958-hunting season by getting a deer. Clara mentioned it in her diary this way, "Hap had to walk for two and a half hours because Red, our horse, had to carry the deer. Then we went for a hayride and had lots of fun."

An example of the problems faced by an outfitter was shown the day Hap got his horse bogged down in a swamp. It took a bit of work but they managed to get him out.

Hap has another story about one of his horses in a swamp. This horse wandered into the swamp on his own and got stuck. Hap found him and with a bit of work managed to get him out. No sooner had he got back to the house, though, then a representative of the government arrived and stopped in. As luck would have it they had a batch of homebrew in progress right beside the stove and the odor would have gave it

Horse stuck in swamp, 1958.

all away. Hap thought quick, rushed out the door and told the gentleman that the horse was stuck in the swamp. He then asked for assistance to free it. By the time they got to the swamp the horse had, by some miracle, managed to free itself. By the time they returned to the house for some coffee, Clara had moved the evidence.

Life was always an interesting challenge, especially guiding and wandering the forests. This had been Hap's dream and step-by-step it was coming true. He found that there was much to learn about packing with horses, and over the years he became an expert at it.

Hap loading packhorse, 1958. Photo courtesy Kyle Foreman.

There were always strange or interesting events taking place at the ranch. Such as the day Hap and Al were walking up to the mill after lunch when they met a cougar on the road. They hurried back and got the rifle and the cougar was still there when they got back. They shot it and the next day Hap took it to town and got $20 for it. They had their picture taken with it by *The Cariboo Observer*.

Cutting ties. That was the theme throughout the winter. When one of the crew left for a job in town, Clara took his place at the mill for two days until the new man, Bill Benz, was hired. Trips to town for fuel, parts and groceries occurred at least once a week. Referring to my mention of strange events taking place at the Bowden Ranch, how about this? On February 8th Hap got a moose. I always thought the season was closed in February. Perhaps they had a special open season in that area.

Some notes from March were, "Made a rag mat for the back door. Took the boys horseback riding today. Hap butchered a steer – first feed of our own beef. We took the rest of the beef to town; we got $100 for 300 pounds." Mixed in with the other notes was a constant one: hauling sawdust from the mill to feed the boundless appetite of the sawdust burner.

April brought the good and the bad. On the good side Hap got a timber wolf and a big beaver. Clara finally got a cooler in the basement. Wild rice was planted along the creek. On the bad side, they tried to go to town and found the road blocked by a slide, but they solved that problem by winching the jeep over it. An even greater problem reared it head on the 29th when Clara started a fire to burn some brush. The fire took off and candled in some treetops before it quieted down. For a time Clara was terrified, convinced she had started a monster forest fire.

Some days were a total loss, such as the day Hap went looking for their horse, Red. He finally arrived back home at noon the following day without a bite to eat. This chasing horses and cattle was a constant around the ranch.

In one of my conversations with Clara I asked, "You were a mighty fine looking young woman, surely you must have had some men give you the eye now and then, didn't you?"

She laughed and then answered, "Well there was one time: I was coming home from town and I got a flat tire. I just got out to look at it when a man came along with a load of hay and offered to change it

Washout just northeast of Beavermouth–just one of many.

for me. He was working on it when a truck stopped and the man hollered at me 'Do you need a hand?' but before I could answer the man working on the tire shouted, 'No! I was here first.'"

I teased Clara a bit more by asking, "Were you ever kissed before you met Hap?"

"No," came her response, "I was slobbered on a couple times but never kissed."

Clara then laughed and made it plain that she had only been joking.

That shut me up; I went back to asking regular-type questions.

On June 1st four people came to fish at the falls and when they returned to the ranch Clara served them sandwiches and coffee. Going by the number of free meals that were served in the Bowden household it seems that they could have made their fortune running a café and to heck with ranching and guiding.

On June 10th a Public Works road crew stayed over at the ranch and when they left the next day they each paid $2. The total of $12 was a nice present for Clara.

Looking ahead to his plans for guiding, Hap hired a plane to fly him in to Maude Lake on the north side of the Quesnel River. This would come back to haunt him later, as he would shortly become hooked on airplanes.

Besides all her housework and taking care of the children Clara

71

found time to do a thousand other errands. The following is just a glimpse of what she did in the last two weeks of June. Planted second round of the garden as the first planting failed from lack of rain. Made Ab a shirt with horses on it: Canned currants, raspberries, huckleberries, saskatoons, gooseberry jam, peas and spinach. As well she canned moose meat. What? Did they open the moose season early again?

New Year's 1959 came in and the temperature dropped. This didn't mean that there was nothing to do. It was a time to sit by the stove, catch up on a lot of reading, get to the overdue letter writing and stoke the fires. When it warmed up Hap got a two-year-old moose. There goes that erratic hunting season again.

What with logging and milling, Hap still found time to measure the distance to Beaver Falls. This was done because they had plans to put a turbine at the bottom of the falls to generate electricity for the ranch. But that was in the future. What was on order at the moment was the construction of a huge barn, so necessary to their guiding

Barn and addition, early 1960s.

dreams. The mill was put to work cutting lumber and the A-frame was lifted 70 feet to hoist the frames. In between days spent on the barn they even found time to tear down an old cabin and build a meat house.

On April 1st they were putting up a frame for the barn when the slip catch got hooked and down she came. Whether there was a connection or not, the hired man, John, packed his things and took off the next day. Hap went after him and found him sitting by the road crying. It seemed that they worked things out because he brought John back to the ranch, but after a week of missing work because of a toothache, John took off to town, sold his rifle for $20 and moved to Williams Lake.

For some reason Hap had trouble getting his vehicle licence renewed, but he had to go to town, so he drove without the licence. When he returned Clara wrote, "Hap went to town without a licence but he didn't get caught."

Clara helped a great deal with the construction of the barn and still found time for her diary entries. Such as the one for April 6th, which stated that the first colt had been born on the ranch, or the note that said Hap had wandered the forest for several days in a fruitless search for his horses. A day later she mentioned that Hap had got a deer and placed it in the new meat house. Darned if the hunting season didn't open early again.

No sooner did Clara get her garden planted than she wrote, "Chickens ate all my peas. Fixed a new chicken coop; they can't get out now."

By mid-July they were putting the roof on the barn, haying and an endless assortment of other jobs. Clara noted, "Hap and Dave went to see Walt Evans and got into his homemade beer. Hap got a deer."

On August 6th Hap bought a new tractor and plow. A few days later Clara was driving the jeep, pulling the tractor out of holes in the meadow. Eventually Hap got ditching powder and blew out a drainage ditch allowing the water level to lower around the meadows. On the 16th Clara added, "My birthday today. Hap doesn't know it. I'll tell him tomorrow." She must have told him, because the next day they went to town and Hap bought her a pair of shoes.

Sometimes there was a need to relax and do a bit of partying. On the 21st she wrote, "We went to McDougals for a party and got home at 4 a.m. I drove because Hap was right out of it." Two days later she added, "Hap is feeling better today."

Back to guiding, Clara noted on October 1st that the men got a moose. Two days later that the men got a black bear. The next day they got another deer and then a moose. On the 6th some satisfied hunters were on their way home.

Hap pointed out that some moose antlers displayed strange characteristics. During the rut the tines are often broken from fighting, but prior to the rut some antlers have long tines while other appear to be absent or broken off, as the following picture shows. I questioned Prince George wildlife biologist Dave King about the cause of this and he claims that these deformations can be caused by damage to the antlers during the formative velvet stage when they are easily damaged. He also states that they can be caused by genetic variations quite common to moose.

Some examples of the guiding results follow: Hap took out four hunters; Ken got a bear and a moose; a few days later Clarence got a

Hap (top) and M.W.Edwards with odd antlers, 1969.

deer; then Norm got a deer and the next day two hunters got their deer; the hunt was capped when Rufus got a big bull moose.

A rather ingenious method was used for packing moose on the horses: they would leave the hide on and then load two front or two hind quarters on a horse by leaving one quarter on each side of the horse. Then they would cut a hole in the hide and hook it over the saddle-horn. This balanced the load perfectly and allowed an easy escape from the pack if the horse fell, as all they had to do was cut the hide where it was hooked over the saddle-horn and the horse was free of its load.

A few problems the Bowdens faced could not be overcome except at great expense. One such problem was the endless rain during the past summer that didn't allow for enough hay to be put up. This was apparent because they had to purchase three loads of hay for $105. This was a goodly sum of money at the time.

That winter produced a rather startling event. Brad was playing outside with the temperature hovering at about 30 degrees below zero when he made the mistake of putting his tongue on the axe blade. Instantly it froze to the cold steel and produced some anxious moments for mom and dad. Hap quickly carried Brad into the house where warm water was applied until the axe blade released its grip.

Clara made the following entries during the month of March, "Kit Knudsen left home at 9 a.m. and got here at supper time. Quite a ski trip (about 14 km) considering he's 75 years old. We went to town and bought the boys a bike. Brad checked the traps and caught a big mink and a small mink."

Then, after noticing that Hap had caught a bug she added, "Hap passed out a couple times; he thought he had it. Didn't sleep all night. I took him to the hospital." A day later she continued, "Hap's back home. I checked the traps and shot one squirrel but when I skinned it I pulled off the tail. Hap got two muskrats and a beaver."

It becomes evident from the foregoing that Clara really was a jack-of-all-trades, such as making four pairs of mitts from an old sweater. Perhaps the strangest remark in her diaries was made on April 12th when she stated, "I didn't do a thing today."

Five days later she wrote, "The boys found all the Easter eggs today including a chocolate one and two Easter chicks as well. Caught four rainbows in the lake today; we're having fish for supper."

Finally in June, "Finished the barn today and went to a cattleman's dance." The next day she added, "Hap has a big head today."

The next purchase was a rotovator and then they built an addition to the barn. At this time they had a herd of 18 cattle. Through August they were haying, picking and canning berries, canning fruit and vegetables from the garden, making jams and jellies and pickles. Everything had to be in order for the coming guiding season. Now that the outfitting business was proving financially successful, the Bowdens sold their timber and concentrated their efforts on guiding.

CHAPTER FOUR
GUIDING

After a few years of trapping and farming, Clara and Hap started Cariboo Mountain Outfitters. This turned into a profit-making business that took up a lot of their time and energy, and gave them a much sought after measure of freedom in return.

The Bowden family, 1958.

The success of this venture is illustrated by the fact that the same hunters returned year after year. In one case a hunter returned nine years in a row. It appears obvious that the Bowdens were doing something right to get that response. Hap is quick to point out that Clara's cooking had something to do with it and after tasting her cooking I have to agree. As well as cooking, Clara had her own guide licence and regularly went along on the hunts. She was, to put it mildly, an essential part of the guiding venture.

The August 29th, 1960 entry was, "Went to town and bought a boat and motor." This was important, as it was needed for their guiding ventures across the Quesnel River. Three hunters arrived on August 30 and the horses were swum across the river in anticipation of the hunt. Four days later they were back with a grizzly bear, which they took to town. They also had a story of a memorable adventure that they shared with *The Cariboo Observer*, and had their pictures taken at the newspaper as well. The article stated: "It took two shots to stop this 500 pound grizzly, along with plenty of iron nerve. Jim Higbee, a contractor from Banning, California, was hunting with Ted "Hap" Bowden in the Cariboo Mountain region. The bear came out of the bush and headed right for Jim who hit the animal about 100 feet away with the first shot from his .30-06. The bear kept coming and Jim fired a second shot, stopping the grizzly 35 feet away. Jim was accompanied on the hunt by Ben Allen and C.P. Mann."

Jim Higbee with a grizzly.

When they went back across the river they immediately got a moose. On the 18th the men returned from the hunt with two grizzlies, a black bear and a moose that they took to the locker in Quesnel. This was a successful hunt to say the least. When the men got home from taking the moose to Quesnel, they found that Clara had shot a black bear that had been bothering the ranch.

By the 22nd they were back from another successful hunt after which they had their pictures taken by *The Cariboo Observer*. As I stated earlier, the media and the Bowdens formed a constant union.

Throughout the many years that they spent guiding, Clara and Hap had a great many memorable experiences. Mixed in with all these adventures was a constant stream of humour. For instance, Hap told me that they had to make everything themselves and that sometimes they were so far from everybody that they even had to create their own children. Judging by some of the people I've known during my lifetime, they must have been a long way back.

Another joke that seems to have grown through the years is the story of the dog. It seems that this trapper had a smart dog that he trained to do countless tasks around the farm. Eventually he even trained the dog to pack all the firewood into the house. Everything went fine until he went on a long trip and forgot to close the door. When he returned two weeks later he were shocked to find the house jammed completely full of firewood. He called for the dog but got no response so he set out on a search. A short time later he found the dog out in the forest. It had fired up his chainsaw and was falling trees to get more firewood.

One story that tickled my funny bone occurred the day Hap set up a hunter on what should have been an easy moose. The hunter fired several shots and the moose ran away. Somewhat embarrassed the hunter turned to Hap and said, "I have good days and bad days and this is one of the last."

Hap has a cute story about a guide that took a black hunter out for bear. As they sat waiting for the bear to come out they were attempting to hide behind some willows. At this point the guide whispered, "You're lucky, it's a lot easier for you to hide than it is for me."

Quick as a whistle the hunter replied, "Yes, but I sure hope it doesn't snow."

Hap also tells the story about the time he guided a 70-year-old man from Louisiana. After nine hours in the saddle they reached camp and Hap dismounted. To his surprise the hunter remained on his horse, prompting Hap to ask, "Haven't you had enough for one day?"

Back came the answer, "Would you please see if you can take me and the saddle off in one piece?"

I enjoyed hearing Hap describe the time one of his hunters fired 12 shots at a moose without hitting it. Desperate for an excuse the hunter exclaimed, "Well that does it; I got rid of all my haywire ammunition; just the good stuff left now."

I find it interesting to dwell on some of the quotes Hap heard during his guiding years. Such as the following made when the hunters were sober:

"Which way did it go?"

"Another jump and it would have had me."

"I must have knocked my sights out of line."

"It looked big in the scope."

"As soon as it roared I decided to get the hell out of there."

"I had to leave because my gun jammed."

"I've never been lost before."

And then there were the quotes made after about six stiff drinks:

"I've never had to fire a second shot."

"No man can out-walk me because I used to carry 100 pounds all day when I was in the Army."

"The bear never lived that can scare me; you show me the biggest grizzly that ever lived and I'll walk up and kick its ass."

"If my gun jammed, I would kill it with my knife."

"You could blindfold me and I still wouldn't get lost."

Hap told me this next story with a twinkle in his eyes so I wouldn't advise anyone to take it to the bank. It seems he was guiding a hunter through the forest when he noticed something strange: the hunter,

A big buck deer.

whose lips were chapped and cracked, would get off his horse occasionally and rub something on his sore lips. On closer inspection Hap noticed that he was rubbing horse droppings on his lips. A short distance along the trail the hunter got down once again and rubbed some bear droppings on his lips. Completely puzzled, Hap asked, "Do you really believe that manure will heal your lips?"

As he mounted his horse the hunter replied, "No, but it sure stops me from licking them."

Getting back to more serious stuff, Hap had a frightening experience when his hunter, Mr. Nelson, got lost. Hap found him the next day by a lake, none the worse for his experience. This was a situation realized by many guides: you just could not take any hunter for granted and had to be aware of what they were up to 24 hours a day.

Clara described an adventure that could have turned into a tragedy, and all of us can take a lesson from this experience. On a trip back from their guide area, the temperature dropped and then a wet snow started falling. Clara was the only person with a slicker so she was all right, but the same was not true for Hap, Brad and Ab. The two boys were about eight and ten at the time. As they made their way along, they kept getting colder and colder, until they finally arrived at a cabin. This is where the rub came in, because Hap had become so hypothermic that he was unable to strike a match to start a fire. Clara got the fire going and eventually got some warmth into the others.

When people live in remote areas they are often forced to improvise, and at times some of these improvisations are memorable. I'm thinking of the time that one of Hap's hunters had trouble with his rifle. When he attempted to remove a spent cartridge from the firing chamber, it froze and could not be removed. Since the fellow needed the gun to hunt, the problem fell to Hap who finally found a solution. He took the lead out of a .22 caliber shell and then placed the barrel of the .22 against the end of the rifle barrel. With the bolt opened on the rifle, he fired the .22 and blew the empty cartridge out of the rifle. Where there is a will there often is a way.

October 21st was a normal guiding day for Hap when he took out two hunters and they came home with a bear and a moose. The next group of hunters left with four deer. The November hunting party left with three deer and four moose, and the early-December group left with a deer and a moose. Little wonder that the news media were always carrying stories of their successful hunts. While reminiscing about stories he had heard around the area many years back, Hap mentioned a trapper and farmer named Henry Gadboy. According to the story Henry got 16 wolves in two days back about 1943. This took place near his ranch at Ben Lake in Skeleton Valley up Beaver Creek. Henry used poison given to him by a game warden and found it to be most effective. The down side of the story was that the wolves froze into the ice on the lake and Henry worked hard to get two per day out of the ice and skin them. It appears that he earned the bounty money he got for the pelts.

Before Christmas 1960, Clara and the boys each got a pair of skates. The next order of business for Hap was to build a skating rink. Many a winter evening was whiled away by the boys in their new-found sport.

There was never a day went by without some project that needed doing. Through the winter months this included another cabin. A fellow named John assisted Hap on this work, but their relationship came to an end when Clara noticed that he had been snooping through things in their bedroom. "What nerve." She commented in her diary.

Clara was pleasantly surprised in March when Hap came home from town with a new propane stove for her birthday. She noted, "I baked bread in my stove; it really turned out good." As if she hadn't had enough on her plate already, Clara was now teaching Brad at home in preparation for school.

After John's dismissal, the next hired hand was a chap named Joe, and he introduced his sense of humour to the Bowdens when he rushed to the door one morning and fired two shots from his rifle. Then he notified everyone that he had shot a cougar. The excitement cooled down considerably, though, when Joe shouted, "April fool."

On May 2nd, Hap and his assistants, Joe and Sonny, took the horses across the river in preparation for a trip. The next day they left on their trip with a boat strapped on to one of the horses. The Bowden's had guided around their property for several years and now wanted to expand.

An elderly trapper named Alf Sundberg owned a fine piece of land to the east of the Quesnel River so Hap paid him a visit. During their conversation Hap asked if he would be interested in selling out and Sundberg declared he was interested. They agreed on a price of

$1000 down and $1000 a year for ten years. Included in the deal were several horses that the Bowdens needed to fulfill their guiding dreams. There was also a rider that Sundberg would stay in the cabin as long as he wanted, and his health would allow.

Horse carrying 350-pound boat.

When Hap went to check out the barn where the horses were kept he received a surprise: the barn had not been cleaned for years, if ever. He grabbed a shovel and was hard at work when Sundberg rushed into the barn and stopped him. "You're going to freeze the horses by taking the manure out," he shouted. There was an element of truth in the statement, as it is true that manure heats, but the poor horses were standing on a sidehill all the time.

When Hap started cleaning out the cabin, Sundberg again interfered and told him he would get sick if he cleaned it too much. According to Hap, Sundberg had a pair of pants that stood up on their own. After years of wiping his hands on them, such as after skinning furs, they were shiny, tough and waterproof.

Another point about this woodsman was the roof of his cabin, which was reminiscent of many trappers' roofs in bygone days.

Hunter, Sundberg and Hap.

Every time he opened a can of any kind he would flatten out the tin can and place it on his roof. After many years of doing so his roof was an endless assortment of different shapes, colours and sizes of cans.

Finally in June 1961 the papers were signed and the deal finalized. The Bowdens had their new guiding area.

After spending five days at the Sundberg place, as it came to be known, Hap and his friends returned home. Then they spent some time making a packsaddle as well as repairing some of the equipment they had got from Sundberg. The expansion of the guiding dreams hoped for by Clara and Hap were quickly taking place.

Sundburg house.

Maude Lake was a regular stopping, fishing and hunting place for the Bowdens, and Clara recalls the day she walked all the way to the lake. She was leading Red as he carried a propane stove into their hunting cabin. On May 14th Clara noted, "Mothers' Day. Ben Miller [an area prospector] came into camp and gave me a beaver tail for soup. I made biscuits on an open fire."

85

Hap bringing a cookstove into the mountains.

The next day she added, "I tried making bread over an open fire. I finished it in the stove. Made beaver tail soup and we caught 20 fish."

On this trip Hap and Clara, Joe and Sonny, built a cabin, a dock for the boat and a corral fence. In between all her other work Clara even found time to put in a garden at the lake. Sixteen days later, with their supplies running low, they returned to the ranch. Hap and his two helpers went back several times to get the Maude Lake cabin ready for the fall hunt. Among the items that were taken to the lake was a power saw and another boat. Then Hap and his helpers worked on the guideline, cutting trail and sizing up the area for hunting.

Clara also had her hands full back at the ranch. Among her regular chores she noted. "I canned 7 quarts and 21 pints of saskatoons, as well as raspberries, strawberries, currants and some meat."

August 17th Clara wrote, "I made myself a birthday cake for dinner. Hap didn't notice until someone said, 'It's a birthday cake.'"

On September 2nd Hap and his helpers, loaded down with supplies, headed across the river with several hunters in tow. The next day he and a hunter took a moose to the locker in town. The following day while Clara was enrolling Brad in school, Hap came along with another moose. A week later the men came back with two caribou. On the 20th two of the hunters assisted Hap out of the mountains to seek medical attention because a moose had gored him. Apparently one of his hunters shot the moose and knocked it down and Hap told him not to shoot again because he could ruin a nice trophy. Instead Hap went to pull out his 9-m.m. handgun to finish it off. His gun got tangled in his clothing, though, and as the moose was charging Hap got off three shots. The moose caught him in the rear with its antlers and By the time they arrived at the doctor's office Hap had a boot full of blood. The doctor gave him a tetanus shot and sewed him up. That same day Hap was back with the hunters ready for more excitement. The next day they brought out another moose.

September 29th brought some excitement when Sonny, their hired guide, came with word that hunter Albert Forrest was lost. The following morning a game warden and three policemen showed up at the Bowden Ranch prepared to join the search. Just as they were ready to leave word came that Albert had been found in a cabin about three miles distant from where he went missing.

Another example of Hap's guiding success was displayed when he left with two hunters for Maude Lake on October 6th and was back the next day with a moose and a deer. A few days later he took another hunter to the lake and brought out another moose.

A successful hunt.

Clara noted on Halloween that Brad and Ab had watched fire-crackers for the first time. Then added, "I baked Hap a birthday cake and bought him a Philishave electric shaver and was he ever pleased."

Two more trips were made into the lake with hunters in November and they brought out a total of four moose and two deer. Surely it wouldn't be an overstatement to say that Cariboo Mountain Outfitters were sending home many satisfied hunters.

Now that Brad had started school in Quesnel, he boarded with a family named Powells. This meant that Hap or Clara had to take him to town every Monday and pick him up every Friday. It was really tough for Brad the first year as Clara repeatedly mentions how home-sick he was.

When 1962 rolled around it found the Bowdens hard at work cutting lumber. Improvements were steady, with a generator delivering a small amount of power to the house. Clara commented that it sure was nice to have an electric light in the basement and arborite for the kitchen. After a severe bout of pneumonia that kept her bedridden for six days, Clara wrote, "The eighth load of lumber went out today and it got stuck on the hill. It cost us $10 to get a tow truck to come from town and pull it out."

No sooner did Clara get over her pneumonia then Brad came down with the measles and it was his turn to stay in bed for several days.

On February 12th word came that old Sundberg had been found dead. Hap was in Vancouver at the time undergoing an operation so he was unable to assist. A neighboring trapper named Jean Crotteau had found him dead in his bed and had determined that he had frozen to death because there was no firewood on the place. Even worse, his cat had eaten a good portion of the body.

The police came to the ranch and took Hap's autoboggan into Maude Lake so that they could recover the body. Clara and Hap felt terrible about his running out of firewood, but like so many other woodsmen, Sundberg was an independent man who never once hinted that he needed help. When Hap mentioned the previous fall that they would get firewood if he needed any, Sundberg replied, "No! I like to get my own wood."

As soon as Hap returned from the hospital, he went with Joe on the autoboggan to Maude Lake to make sure everything was in order after Sundberg's death. While they were gone Rosie calved and Clara made a statement that troubles me, "Rosie calved and I carried water to her. It's a nice calf even if it is a bull." Ouch!

When March arrived the frost penetrated the ground and froze the newly dug waterline. Hap called for help and the Public Works came and tried to thaw it out with steam, but instead of thawing the pipe, they melted it. This meant they were back to packing water until the ground thawed. Oh! The joy of wilderness living.

In April Hap again flew to Maude Lake a couple times. There was no doubt that he wanted an airplane with which to fly his hunters into the backcountry. On his second flight he experienced what can be enough to make an individual give up on flying – extreme motion sickness. In Hap's case it didn't work as he had already made up his mind that he was going to fly.

Just an example of the endless chores faced by these enterprising people was demonstrated on May 6th when they spent two days searching to find all their horses. Then they had the job of shoeing and branding the animals before swimming them across the river in preparation for the next trip. Meanwhile, Clara, who was used to staying alone at the ranch, noted, "I shot a skunk in the chicken house and buried it." The importance of getting the skunk immediately cannot be overstated, as there are few animals that can kill a dozen chickens faster than a skunk.

When September rolled around Ab started school, so now they had two children to haul to and from school every week. This left Clara free to assist on the hunts and over the next two weeks Clara mentions five moose coming out across the river. On October 23rd, they got to Sundberg's after dark, yet the next day they had a moose and the following day they had a bear.

Again, two hunters came on November 17th and left two days later with two deer. Then Hap's assistant guide came from Maude Lake with two deer and one moose. There can be no doubt that Hap and Clara had found their calling.

When January 1963 turned the corner, Clara was busy knitting sweaters and making shoelaces. Hap had built a smokehouse and was busy smoking meat. Then it was off to Vancouver where they picked up a Volkswagen.

The highlight for February was a trip to Sundberg's where they looked at the possibility of building an airstrip. There goes that airplane idea again. Then they carried on to Maude Lake where they found several trees down around their cabin, including one that fell on the outhouse.

Taking the children to and from school was a continuous and trying task. Sometimes they had to go to town on the early morning frost and then stay in town until late evening when the frost would tighten up the road again. On one trip into town after high winds, they were forced to take seven trees off the road in order to be able to continue their journey.

The down side of living far from town was that they were distant from medical attention. This was at times trying, to say the least: such as the time that they both came down with a bug and spent several days in bed. For a while Hap's temperature hovered at 104 degrees.

As soon as they recovered from the flu, they butchered a pig. Then spent some time curing pork and roasting a hindquarter. But the best was yet to come when Clara made stuffed ribs for dinner. I drool just thinking about it, because I well remember my mother baking ribs after we butchered hogs at home. So help me I have never tasted store-bought meat that came close to being comparable.

A break from cutting trail, 1963.

During April, Hap's father came to visit and on the 23rd they swam 11 horses across the river and again headed for Sundberg's. Several beaver traps were set and a trail was cut to Edwards Creek. As for skinning beaver Clara noted, "What a job!"

When they returned to the ranch, the men went to work falling timber again. This was when a strange thing happened. Ab, who was only seven years old, was falling trees as well. Somehow one of the trees he fell managed to land a glancing blow off grandpa's head. He was rushed to the hospital in Quesnel where he received 13 stitches. Did he survive, you ask? You bet, and apparently he was a lot more observant after that when the young lads were up and about. As to whether that stopped the boys from falling trees, that was answered just two weeks later when Clara's diary entry stated, "Hap and the boys fell cottonwood trees to make three-inch planks for the barn floor."

That summer, besides all the regular work of haying, gardening, canning and lumbering, there was a whole parcel of new projects. They put cement posts under the barn, and then they returned to Sundberg's, and on to Little Maude Lake where they built another cabin. They even put in plastic pipe so there was running water to the cabin, built a woodshed and toilet. In between all their chores they found time to catch and smoke 21 fish. There was no time for boredom at Cariboo Mountain Outfitters.

The August 19th entry was, "Hap and Walt left for Quesnel with pack horses. Brownie put on a show and bucked them off twice." The next day she added, "Hap and Walt came back with the pack train and heavy loads."

During the trip to Maude Lake, they put shakes on the woodshed roof, dug a well and cut on a trail toward Cariboo Mountain. In early September they brought two hunters into the area and by the following day their hunters had a bear and a moose. After the hunt was over, work continued on the trail until the 18th when they reached an alpine meadow on Cariboo Mountain. This was of great significance because now they were up high where they would find caribou and an abundance of large buck deer.

It was while they were tent camping cutting this trail that they were bothered by a big black bear that came and got into their meat cache. The next night after they had retired, Hap was trying to stay awake in case the bear came back. At his side Clara was in dreamland. Suddenly the big bear walked right in front of their tent and headed for the meat cache. Hap states that he barely nudged Clara and she was instantly awake. Then she held the flashlight on the bear while Hap shot it at point blank range.

October 1st found Hap and an assistant guide heading back to Sundberg's. Two days later all the hunters had their moose and the pack train headed back home. The importance of all the trails they had cut was evident and paying dividends.

The Bowden's had another project going at this same time. They hired a crew to put a dam across Beaver Creek just above the falls. This was necessary to keep a head of water for constant flow to the turbine, which was to be put below the falls to generate electricity for the ranch.

This was a tremendous undertaking because a flume had to be built to carry the water to a trommel where it dropped 70 feet to the

Hap and author at Beaver Falls. The dam is still sound 40 years later.

turbine at the bottom of the falls. As well, power poles had to be erected to deliver the power to the ranch about a kilometer distant. Two transformers were also required to push the power that far without too much loss. When the power project was completed it generated 12,000 watts and allowed two large floodlights to be left on at nights. This lit-up area in the middle of nowhere led to the ranch being called Bowdenville by some local pilots.

When January 1964 came into view, it found Clara busy writing letters to hunters. She noted, "We got a deposit from three hunters; it sure came in handy."

When the Easter break came along the family gathered up the boys and headed back to Sundberg's. They arrived in the area to find that there was too much snow. Reluctantly, with the boys already missing school, they headed back from the area that was fast becoming their first love.

It was the middle of May when they next made their way back to Sundberg's. The men spent the next several days cutting trail to the Swift River while Clara stayed at the cabin planting garden and skinning beavers. As soon as the trail was complete they returned home. It must be pointed out that their trips had to be planned to coincide with the boys' days off from school. This often meant coming out of the mountains on Fridays and going back in on Mondays or Tuesdays.

After the boys were dropped off at school, it was back to Sundberg's with supplies, where Clara noted that they had seen a black and a grizzly bear along the trail. Throughout the coming years this family would see a lot of grizzlies.

The children grew up fast on Bowden ranch, as evidenced by the fact that Hap was teaching Ab—at the tender age of eight–to drive the tractor. The boys also helped with gardening and a multitude of other chores.

Throughout the years the Bowdens had terrible luck with their dogs. Just a few years earlier they had run over a dog while putting their vehicle in the garage, now their one-year-old dog, Flash, jumped into the mower blade and had its

Grizzlies eating salmon.

back legs cut so severely that it had to be put down. Another painful loss was experienced when one of their horses died from tapeworms. Hap says they had no idea the horse was in trouble until it was too late.

Hap was always one to keep in shape, and this was emphasized in July when he put up a set of acrobat rings that he had become proficient on many years earlier. This would come back to bite him several years later as we shall see.

On August 1st they were taking supplies into Sundberg's when they ran into a grizzly that attacked them and Hap had no choice but to shoot the bear. Clara noted that the excitement was too much for Ab who broke down crying, terrified that the bear was going to get his daddy. On this trip they took a boat in to Sundberg Lake and built a corral. Clara wrote, "We caught 13 fish in Victoria Creek and smoked them. We also saw six deer."

The March 5th edition of Quesnel's newspaper *The Cariboo Observer* carried a brief summary of Hap's life. This was just one of countless interviews Hap had with the media throughout the years and it detailed several of the stories mentioned here.

One of Hap's greatest interests was observing game and thereby becoming a better guide. He told me of an observation that was gained from a Native Indian who had spent many years in the forests. It concerned the reason for the bell on a moose. This gentleman suggested that a person take note when a moose lifts its head after feeding underwater. Often the moose's nose and the bottom tip of the bell will not come out of the water when the moose lifts its head. The reason for this is so that the water will quietly run off the nose and bell and thus allow the moose to hear approaching danger.

Hap and his hunters made another interesting observation one day as they rode along a trail on horseback. Suddenly they spotted a grizzly and cub on the trail ahead of them. The mother grizzly sensed their presence and somehow got the cub to jump up on her back. As the men watched in amazement the sow ran away along the trail with the cub up on her back hanging on for dear life.

CHAPTER FIVE
CARIBOO MOUNTAIN

N ow that the Bowdens had reached the top of Cariboo Mountain they had opened up a new door in their lives. For here they were going to secure many fine trophies for their clients. After the usual busy summer, it was time to take a hunting party to Sundberg's for the start of the 1964 guiding season. They arrived at base camp and the next day the family went fishing to a small nearby lake where they made a fine catch. Ab insisted on carrying the fish back to camp so he placed them in a gunnysack tied to the horse's saddle. As they made their way through the forest toward camp it got dark. When they arrived at camp they were shocked to find that the gunnysack had snagged on some branches and torn open with the result that all their fish had been lost in the forest. Just as a joke Hap said to Ab, "You're going to have to take a flashlight and go back and get those fish." Ab took him seriously and burst into tears, terrified at the thought of wandering alone in the forest after dark. Hap let Ab know that he was just fooling and the issue was quickly sorted out, but to this day that tiny lake is known locally as Gunnysack Lake.

Two days later the Bowdens took three hunters into this same area. On their second day they went fishing, caught fish and ate them for supper. By the time their hunt ended these men left with three moose and a bear. The next group of hunters stayed five days and left with three moose. On October 1st they left home with four hunters and as was often the case, had a terrible time finding the horses after they crossed the river. Once back in the wilderness it took two days to get three moose and two more days to get the fourth moose and bring them out to town.

On October 11th they were heading back to base camp with a new group of hunters when they got two moose on the trail. The packhorses were loaded and had just started out with the meat when they heard a shot and learned that one of their hunters already had another moose.

October 21st saw them heading back to Sundberg's and within a day they had three deer and a moose. Time was spent enjoying some fishing and then another moose was taken. The trip was over and another group of satisfied hunters were on their way home. Yet another example of a superb hunt occurred two weeks later when their hunters got three buck deer the first day and two moose the second. It appears obvious that Hap and Clara had found their station in life.

The amount of time spent looking for horses was considerable, but small in comparison to one long search they made for some of their missing calves. This search started on November 26th and the next day they found five calves. On December 3rd they found two more and sighted another that was too wild to approach. They got the last calf home on the 6th of January.

The joys of wilderness living were again demonstrated in April 1965 when Clara attempted to go to town to get the boys. She ended up stuck in a mud hole and had to jack the vehicle out herself. A week later she tried again only to find a slide had blocked the road.

The fortitude shown by this family was again displayed a week later when Hap and his assistant guide tried to go back to Sundberg's. They found Beaver Creek high and wild with the bridge washed out at Beavermouth, so they had to swim on horseback. One way or another they got the job done.

Something that needs to be pointed out was the method used to get the horses across the Quesnel River. The Bowdens would take one horse across with a rope tied to their boat. Once the first horse was across it was a simple matter to

Swimming horses across the Quesnel River, 1960s.

drive the other horses across the river, as they would always try to join the first horse.

97

Their guiding business grew, and so Hap started taking hunters on spring hunts for bears. On May 10th he started out for Sundberg's with a hunter and they got a big black bear on the way in. This was another short but successful hunt and a means of extending the guiding season income.

A surprising and troublesome problem arose in June when Hap returned from a trip to Vancouver only to find a Forestry 242 order pinned to his door. It read as follows:

"To Mr. Ted Bowden, Box 99, Quesnel, BC:

This is to advise that you have five horses grazing in trespass on Crown Range in the vicinity of lot 9158 Cariboo. This range is under permit to Mr. Arbea and Mr. Callhan. Please have the horses removed to Crown Range as granted to you by permit, or to your own private land prior to June 15, 1964. Failure to remove the horses by the above date will leave the department no alternative but to do so, and bill you for expenses incurred."

The letter was signed by Deputy Ranger Steve Marynovich.

Hap was furious with the order because he had been leasing the area for the previous three years and assumed he had priority there. The worst rub was that Hap would have had to move his horses back and forth across the river before and after every hunt, whereas previously he had been able to leave them across the river ready for the next hunt.

To make a long story short, this battle went on for some time and even involved the then Minister of Lands and Forests, Ray Williston. After a great deal of time and correspondence, this matter was finally brought to a successful conclusion when Hap was given a portion of his former lease. The parties came to agreement and a fence was built between their grazing leases.

As I worked with Steve Marynovich in the Forest Service and knew him to be a cool, collected chap, I questioned him about the event. He told me that when he confronted Hap about the trespass, Hap told him, "Listen here! I used to be a boxer and I could kick your ass if I wanted."

To that Steve replied, "I'm sure you could, but that wouldn't solve the problem; your horses would still be in trespass."

Perhaps the reader can now understand why one of Hap's favorite sayings is, "The wheel is round; if it doesn't want to roll, we push it."

Once the range dispute was settled, another horse named Queenie was purchased and added to the herd, which eventually totaled 18. Often it took 14 or 15 head of horses to carry everyone as well as all the provisions. It also took all the horses to carry out the meat after a successful hunt, especially if they managed to bag four moose – a considerable weight to carry out of the mountains.

And what were the boys up to during the long summer days? Why they were doing what most young lads dream of doing: fishing, swimming, building forts and riding horses. Surely it is not hard to visualize the endless opportunities for adventure that were available to these young lads.

As to the statements made by some experts that wolves don't harm horses. I wouldn't recommend that anyone try to convince

Hap leading the pack train.

Hap about this, because he lost a colt to wolves in 1964. The photo shows how the wolves brought the colt down by attacking it from behind. There is no way to be certain but Hap believes he got the guilty party a few days later. Was the colt wasted, you ask? Not completely, because Clara got back to making colt hide vests again.

Brad and Ab with the colt the wolves killed, 1964.

Another one-sided battle occurred to one of Hap's horses shortly after he sold it. This horse was a registered quarter horse named Nazko Jack that Hap traded to Lynn Ross, the man who took the buffalo into the Fort Nelson area. Lynn had the horse just a short time before it was killed by a grizzly bear.

An inkling of what Clara was up to, besides her endless chores, was noted in her diary of August 8th: "I picked lots of raspberries and then I started to make Hap a beaver and moose hide vest. I also fixed his lamb hide vest."

One diary entry read, "We went to Beavermouth and while we were gone the boys baked me a cake." There was no mention about whether it was edible or not.

When August rolled around, the Bowdens were back in the mountains building fences and cutting trails. This was a necessary part of upgrading experienced by all guides and outfitters. Hap emphasized the obvious, "Nothing sits still in nature; it either moves ahead or else it moves backwards." I know from experience that this certainly applies where trails are concerned; if you neglect them they quickly disappear.

Hap and Clara got right into the 1965-hunting season by getting their hunters two moose in the first two days. Clara noted, "We took

Guide Clara with two elated hunters, 1965.

the moose to town today. Everything was closed so the men couldn't get a beer. There's a beer shortage because of the strike."

Immediately after this hunt Clara and Hap returned to Cariboo Mountain where they continued cutting trail. Their first night at camp they were visited by a bear that came into camp and took some bacon and other meat. The following night it returned and took another load of goodies. In an effort to stop this sneaky devil before he cleaned them out of food, Hap made a gun-set, but it was not successful.

The next day Hap's assistant guide took two hunters and their moose to town. When Hap got back to his truck after the hunt was over he noticed that his new .300 Weatherby rifle had been taken from where he had hidden it under some material in the vehicle. It had been stolen, and this was a big loss that really bothered Hap. In fact to this day he clearly recalls the serial number of the rifle as 32171.

On the 21st they again returned to Sundberg's with hunters. A week later they were back home with two moose and two deer. On their next trip they took four hunters and were back in five days with four moose. They left for the guideline again on October 10th and the hunters shot a moose on the way in, just at dusk. The next morning they returned to get the moose only to find that a grizzly had found the carcass and buried it. This sort of thing goes with the territory in a guide's life, and shows that one cannot be too careful about approaching a carcass after it has been left for any period of time.

One thing that was a constant on a Bowden moose hunt was a cake for the first person to get their moose. But on one trip the first successful moose hunter was a rather pompous chap. As soon as he got his moose he really laid into the other hunters, making it clear to them that he was the superior hunter. But the joke was on him when Clara handed him his trophy cake, because written across it were the appropriate words, "Number one bull-shooter."

World champion bull-shooter.

After yet another successful guiding trip, Hap took eleven heifers and one steer to a cattle sale; even the ranch was finally starting to pay dividends.

And then there was a rather memorable situation that arose one day on the ranch. One of their cows gave birth and then prolapsed. Several hours were spent in an effort to keep it in but to no avail. Hap finally solved the problem by putting a large bottle of sand in on top of it. That did the job, and when the animal went to market, they even got paid for the weight of the sand and the bottle.

Always ready with another round of humour, Hap had another quaint story concerning a trapper that went into a grocery store to purchase some badly needed vittles. Once in the store he checked his money supply, which was almost nothing. Desperate, he asked a clerk if he could purchase half a head of lettuce. Somewhat taken aback, the clerk said he would check with his boss. The clerk found the boss and said to him, "Believe it or not, some asshole wants to buy half a head of lettuce."

No sooner had he spoken the words then the boss pointed behind the clerk, who then whirled around to find that the trapper had followed him. Without missing a beat, the clerk continued, "And this fine gentleman would like the other half."

Hap spent many an hour relating guiding tales to me and impressed upon me just how hilarious some of the hunters' antics really were. Such as the American that arrived and wanted to "get with it." As it was too late in the day to saddle up and head for the guideline, Hap decided to take this chap by vehicle to a little used area off the beaten track. The instant Hap stopped the vehicle the hunter was out the door and fired five shots into the air from his high-powered rifle. Hap rushed around the vehicle and asked the man what he was doing. Whereupon the hunter replied, "I like to get the game up on their feet and let them know I'm in the area." As the

Clara and a hunter fording a stream.

hunter considered himself a good sportsman, he figured it was only fair to give the animals a sporting chance.

Hap tells the story about one of his hunters that he asked to follow a well-marked trail. At the same time, Hap was working the woods off to the side in an effort to drive an animal to the hunter. Suddenly he heard the hunter hollering in an excited manner so he rushed through the woods to his side. When queried, the hunter pointed to some tracks in the snow and said, "Man these Canadian boys are tough, just look at these tracks – some damned fool has been out hunting barefoot." After a quick glance at the tracks, Hap explained to the hunter that the tracks were made by a three-year-old black bear. After a moment of embarrassment, the hunter, who was a good sport, broke up with such laughter that he almost fell out of the saddle.

And then there was the evening after a long day's hunt that the hunters invited Hap to their cabin for a drink. Hap assured them that he would be along after he tended to the horses. When he finished the chores he walked to their cabin where he was handed a water glass plum full of whiskey. At once Hap stated, "Good heavens man, I couldn't possibly drink all that; it would kill me."

The hunter laughed and then said, "Why hell, man, that can't hurt you; I've been drinking a quart of this stuff every day for the last five years and it hasn't done me any harm."

At that point the other hunter, who had a bad case of the shakes, spoke up, "Aw de hell, man, quit your bragging; I spill more than you drink."

To this the first hunter replied, "Don't worry about him, he's an undertaker and he'll be the last to let you down."

Clara and Hap not only taught their children to always have a good sense of humour, they also taught them how to survive and take care of themselves. My favorite story concerns Brad and an event that took place in January 1966 when he was 11 years old. The temperature dropped to −30 degrees so school was cancelled. This left Brad in Quesnel with nothing to do. Just a week earlier Brad had asked his father for some spending money, but instead of money, he got some valuable instructions. Hap informed his son that money had to be earned; then suggested a method of doing so. He told Brad to watch for walkways that were snowed in when he was in Quesnel, then to knock on the doors of those houses and ask if they would like their sidewalks shoveled. To this Brad asked, "How much should I charge?"

"Don't worry about that," Hap replied, "just tell them to pay you what they think it is worth."

That weekend when Brad returned home from school he was the proud owner of $7. He then informed his folks that one of the houses he visited belonged to the local magistrate. When Brad finished shoveling the snow, the magistrate – obviously impressed with his entrepreneurial spirit – gave him $5 and told him to open a bank account, which he did. The $7 Brad had earned was the equivalent of a man's wages for half a day at that time. There can be no doubt that Brad was proud of himself.

Yet another example of the boys taking care of themselves and each other occurred when they were playing along the stream that meandered through the ranch. With the temperature hovering around –20 degrees, the boys were walking along on the ice when Ab suddenly broke through into the icy water. Brad instantly came to his rescue by grabbing a willow that grew along the bank and holding the tip of it down so that Ab could grab it. Then he helped his brother out of the water and back to the house where his already frozen clothing was removed. Clara and Hap were not only shocked, but also eternally grateful to their eldest son.

Ab with the fisher he and Brad caught and skinned.

March brought a strange occurrence when one of their colts became paralyzed and Hap had to put it down. Was it wasted, you ask? Not completely because Clara made Hap another colt hide vest.

To give an idea of how advanced the boys were at an early age I want to point out that they checked Clara's trap line and found a fisher in a trap. When the boys got home they were extremely excited and who can blame them. Then they even went one further and skinned the fisher. Not too bad for two lads aged nine and eleven.

In early April 1966 a series of claims were filed along the Quesnel River. As Hap was always looking for a chance to make a dollar, he hired on and spent many a day staking for others. In total 3500 claims were filed in a six-month period.

Hap's dad stopped for his usual visit in April and when they went to take him back to Quesnel, Trowler Creek was washed out. On the other side of the creek, a Boy Scout leader and his troupe were intent on heading out into the forest. A quick discussion was held and the two groups exchanged vehicles, then continued on their respective ways. One way or another they always seemed to get the job done.

On the 26th of April Hap was prospecting his claims when a bear attacked him. Probably he just got too close to the mother who was trying to protect her cubs. Only after he shot her did Hap realize there were cubs involved. He took the cubs home where the boys immediately adopted them. It was love at first sight, but the cubs could not stay. Two weeks later they were shipped to Al Oeming's Game Farm in Alberta.

Hap and Clara staked two more mineral claims in May and then it was back to Sundberg's with a bear hunter. Clara stated that the hunter saw a black bear but when he went to shoot, two shells came up at the same time and jammed the rifle. If the truth be known, it may well be that the hunter got buck fever and worked the action twice without letting it travel the full distance. I know from experience that rifles get blamed for a lot of things that are not their fault.

Brad and Ab with bear cubs, 1966.

105

During the month of June, Hap took time to go on a prospecting trip with Ed Chase and a well-known bush pilot named Tom Corless. They traveled up the chain of lakes from Fort St. James to Takla Lake where they checked out the area for copper. Convinced that it was low-grade ore, they gave up on the venture and returned home. Instead Hap and Clara staked another 34 claims in the Quesnel River area for others, and then took a geologist to the area to inspect them.

At this same time they started having problems with their power because gravel was getting into the turbine. Between gravel and leaves they were to have a great deal of trouble in the following years. In fact, after all the expense they went to in getting the dam and turbine set up, they only got about one full year of service from it.

Not only was Brad proving his worth around the ranch, what with running the tractor and the rotovator at the ripe old age of 11, but that year he also managed to bag his first deer. The boys learned so much in their early years, but this should not be surprising, because in spite of all the jokes that were made about farm boys, many were light years ahead of their city peers in general knowledge.

A good example of the boys' willingness to take responsibility was shown when they got off the school bus at Beavermouth. A rancher from across the river told them that the Bowden horses were back at their grazing area instead of being up at Sundberg's with Clara and Hap. Immediately the boys assumed that the horses had run away and left their parents stranded. This moved them to action. They crossed the river, caught the horses and then rode them bareback all the way to Sundberg's; arriving late at night in the dark. But Clara and Hap were not at Sundberg's, instead they were back at the ranch. When they learned what happened they rushed toward Sundberg's where they found the boys hiking back out and about fives miles into their journey.

Clara and Hap were so impressed with the boys that they took them along on a September hunt where they got a first-hand look at a hunter in action. One of the hunters got a shot at a moose and lost it. Then he was so disgusted that he only paid half the price of the hunt. Perhaps an elderly guide hit it pretty close when he said, "You get all kinds of people out there, and some of them aren't so nice to deal with." Sometimes it appears that hunters expect the guide to have their animals tied to trees in anticipation of their arrival.

The majority of hunters were extremely delighted, such as the next

Hap and Clara in Porter Creek cabin, 1968. Photo courtesy Kyle Foreman.

three hunters to reach Cariboo Mountain. They left with three deer and a moose with a 46-inch spread. And then there was the hunter named Larry Chaves who came for a hunt in 1968 and left with the record grizzly of the year. When the Bowdens needed references they sure didn't have any trouble finding them.

For a few years in the late 60s, Hap hired an assistant guide named Dale Ethier. Dale, who wrote *Wilderness Captive*, left the Quesnel area after the 1968 guiding season where he took top honors for the most trophy awards of the season. The next year he set up his own guiding operation on Takla Lake north of Fort St. James, BC. His guiding days were short lived, though, because of a nagging back problem that forced him out of the guiding business.

Hap and Clara have an interesting story concerning a grizzly bear. This animal broke into one of their cabins at Porter Creek and Swift River by gaining entry through a window. On its rampage through the cabin it started biting into all the cans that were available. At some point it took a massive bite out of a Raid can and got the surprise of its life. The unfolding story was easy to read when the Bowdens

Larry Chaves' world-record grizzly, 1968.

entered the cabin, because there was a trail of bear droppings from the can across the cabin and out the window. This was one bear that never came back.

The foregoing may be an asset to people removed from civilization who are troubled by bears. It strikes me that it makes more sense to startle a troublesome bear by letting it bite into a can of Raid or mosquito dope rather than shoot it. This is especially true if it is a sub-adult bear that simply doesn't know any better. Perhaps smearing a bit of cold bacon grease on the can would assist the problem bear in finding the can.

Hap's greatest scare, though, came on a grizzly hunt when he set the hunter up on a bear at close range. Perhaps the hunter experienced buck fever, because he fired a shot and wounded the bear, which immediately took cover. Then the hunter wanted to follow it but Hap checked him by insisting that the bear be allowed a few minutes to die. As they stood there waiting they heard a noise and realized that the wounded bear had circled and was attacking from the side. The hunter took off and left Hap to face the bear all by his lonesome. It took two bullets, but Hap put the bear down to stay. As soon as the hunter realized the bear was dead he showed new interest in the hide.

Clara recalled the day in May when they started a grass fire to clean up the area around Sundberg's. The fire got away and burned down their cookhouse. This meant that 12 years of Clara's diary and many days of hard work had just gone for naught.

Hap has another story of near disaster in the forest. It concerns hornets. While attempting to take his pack train across the Swift River, they disturbed a nest of hornets and all hell broke loose. Apparently Clara's horse went by traveling at great speed and Hap

Mr. Gorman with the grizzly that charged.

shouted at her to find out what was going on. Before she could answer another bunch of horses went flying by. Hap suggests that people have no idea what a horse can do until they watch it perform after it has been stung inside the nose by a hornet. This just goes with the territory, though, and if you don't believe me, just ask any guide.

Clara and Hap offered an interesting footnote to this story by saying that the next time they arrived at this same spot they found three deer standing out in the water and two wolves waiting patiently on the shore. The wolves departed as soon as they arrived.

Now I want to change pace and bring someone else into this story.

People who are familiar with the Barkerville and Wells areas of BC have probably heard of a prospector called "The Lucky Swede." During the winter of 1981/82, I spent some time working in that area with three other fellows for the Ministry of Forests. In the evenings we sometimes went to the hotel in Wells where we played pool and drank a few beers to while away the time. On our first evening at the hotel we immediately noticed an old-timer seated alone at a table, so we asked him to join us at our table and he readily accepted. We introduced ourselves and then he informed us that he was known throughout the area as "The Lucky Swede," a person I had heard about from other woodsmen and prospectors.

Throughout our stay in Wells, this gentleman–probably in his seventies–entertained us with endless stories about his life as a prospector and the origin of his nickname. Contrary to what his nickname implies Lucky (he didn't tell us his real name that I recall) was not a Swede, having arrived in Canada in 1927 from Norway. For a few years he worked as a logger in Manitoba, but decided that place was too cold for him so he came west to BC in 1929.

No sooner had he arrived, though, then he heard stories of fabulous wealth in the form of gold, just waiting to be picked up off the ground. He worked the West Kootenays for a while and then, just as so many others had done before him, headed for the famous Cariboo. His first claim to success occurred near the town of Lytton, where he found gold on a stream called Coyote Creek. As soon as his poke was full Lucky walked to Lillooet where–drawn by an urge that haunted him throughout his life – he stopped at a beer parlor. A few drinks loosened his tongue and in a matter of hours everyone in town knew about his strike. When Lucky's head cleared he returned to the creek to find the entire area had been staked, so once again he moved on.

During the summer of 1933 Lucky first arrived in Barkerville, where he went to work as a hydraulic miner. By 1936 he again decided to go on his own and after panning for a few weeks, he found a six and one-quarter ounce nugget. Gold was selling for $26 an ounce at the time, so Lucky went to Barkerville and sold the nugget. This was the origin of "The Lucky Swede" tag that was to stay with him for the rest of his life.

One of the stories Lucky told us (several times to be exact) concerned a Finlander he stayed with for a time. This fellow was not overly ambitious, so rather than cut and split his own firewood, he used to swipe it from a neighbor. The neighbor finally figured out where his wood was going, so he set a trap. He hollowed out a stick of firewood and filled the center with a stick of dynamite and a short fuse. One evening Lucky and the Finn returned to the cabin and set about lighting the fire so that they could enjoy a quiet evening at home. The fire was also needed to keep the crock of beet wine from getting too chilled. No sooner did the fire get going, though, then there was a tremendous explosion during which the lids flew off the stove, the stove door flew open and ashes blew all over the cabin. As well, the beet wine was evenly distributed all over the cabin, giving it the appearance of a slaughter house. According to Lucky, the Finn got his own firewood after that.

Far from living the life of Riley, though, The Lucky Swede was not always lucky. He told us about hardships he had endured; such as the time he spent an entire winter living on nothing but flour, a bit of rice and wild rabbits.

There is what I consider to be an important reason for bringing The Lucky Swede into the Bowden story, and that has to do with art. Perhaps many people are unaware that Lucky was an artist who spent a great deal of time drawing pictures. During the summer of 1971, Hap and Clara decided to clean up an old mining building atop Cariboo Mountain that they used as a guide outfitters' cabin for many years. This was a tedious and dirty job in that the entire floor was covered with several inches of packrat droppings that had accumulated over the many years that the building had sat idle. Almost as if they were being rewarded for their efforts, they made an interesting discovery. Hanging on a wall was a drawing of a woman, naked from the waist up. Plainly written across the drawing is the signature "The Lucky Swede.Written across the back of the drawing are the words, "Drawn in the Wells Hotel–1960.

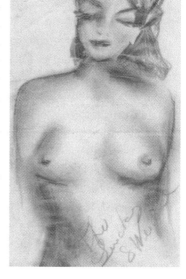

Drawing by the Lucky Swede.

After consultation with Clara and Hap, I have forwarded the original copy of this drawing to the Barkerville Museum where it rightfully belongs.

There is another source of information regarding the Lucky Swede that came to me from Darrel Williams of Prince George. Darrel was raised in the Wells/Barkerville area and knew The Lucky Swede for many years. Darrel knew that he was an excellent artist and added

Hap calling moose. Photo courtesy Klye Foreman.

that Lucky was even hired to draw a mural on the wall of the Jack O'Clubs hotel.

Getting back to the Bowdens, a big change came to their ranch in 1971 when Hap got his pilot's licence and bought a Taylorcraft airplane. Within a year they built two airstrips at the ranch and another at the Sundberg place. These were but the first of four airstrips they built throughout the years.

Hap tells a story about a scare he got with their first plane when he was flying back from Salt Spring Island to Quesnel with his brother-in-law, Dave Pallot. One of the fuel tanks stopped the flow of gas somehow and this forced him to fly on the other tank. After flying on the same tank for a while, Hap realized that the plane was becoming unbalanced with one wing much heavier than the other. He decided it was best to play it safe, so he found a place to land where a road intersected a meadow and brought the plane down safely. A quick check found the problem: a cork spacer under the gas tank lid that had deteriorated and allowed a vacuum to stop the flow of fuel. By the time the men fixed the problem it was too late to fly so they took refuge in a nearby guide's cabin for the night. This created its own story, in that Hap was sound asleep when he was awakened by something pulling out his hair. Just enough moonlight was coming through the window for Hap to make out the form of a packrat right beside his head. It was pulling out his hair, probably to build a nest with. Hap swung at the animal and missed, but as it made its way across the floor, Dave gave it a kick that sent it right up to the ceiling. Then they were left to sleep in peace for the rest of the night.

Somehow Ab must have inherited his father's love of pushing the envelope because he started to use the airplane to go to school while his folks were out guiding. It was not uncommon for some farmer to find Ab landing in his fields because the area of Quesnel was fogged in. After landing he would have to hitchhike to school as best he could. Even though he didn't have a pilot's licence that didn't stop him from flying.

Hap and Taylorcraft airplane, 1974.

Hap recalls the day they were guiding at Sundberg's when Ab flew in and dropped a package of mail and supplies to them. Apparently one of the horses was standing with his head hung almost asleep when the bag landed on a piece of tin right beside it. Then there was a transition from slumber to wild bronco in two seconds flat.

Always looking for a new challenge or venture, the Bowdens purchased 320 acres of land on Maude Creek for $2500, then resold it for $10,000. Sounds like a good deal, doesn't it? Well the rub came when the new owner logged $300,000 worth of timber off it and eventually sold it for another $300,000.

As for the airplane, they did find use for it on the guideline. In fact, Hap states that he often flew game out with it. But he didn't use it to haul passengers because it was not insured for that use.

A point that merits mentioning concerns moose and bears. Almost any guide can confirm the devastating effect black bears can have on moose populations, since they see the results of calf moose kills. What is sometimes not well known is that even a yearling black bear will attempt to injure a calf moose and then bide its time until the mother of the injured or dead calf leaves the area. Then the bear will move in to feed. In other similar cases I have personally witnessed attempts by the bears to catch these calves, although they were not successful because I intervened.

113

Hunter Gordon Gorman with large black bear, 1971.

Injuries are a fact of life when involved in something as active as guiding with horses through rugged country. Although the Bowdens were generally lucky, they had their moments. I'm thinking of the day they were making their way along when one of the hunters allowed his horse to crowd a pack-horse too closely. The packhorse lashed out with its hind feet and struck the hunter on the lower leg resulting in a compound fracture of the tibia. The hunter was in agony and the train came to a sudden stop. Hap managed to get through on his radio and after an agonizing wait a chopper arrived just before dark. The man was flown to Quesnel hospital where the pilot was forced to make an illegal night-time landing.

Clara and Hap have so many memories to share. Such as the time they were returning home from a Guide's Convention when they found the road blocked by fallen trees caused by a severe windstorm.

Clara cutting trees, 1972.

Clara immediately got out the axe and went to work chopping the trees off the road. I asked Hap if she really did cut the trees and he responded with, "You bet she did; she could do anything."

Another investment that seemed necessary was the purchase of 58 acres of land on the Quesnel River at a place called Twenty-mile along the Quesnel-Hydraulic Road. The Bowdens needed this place because it offered them easier access to the remotest part of their guideline. Actually it saved them about a 35-km ride on horseback.

There is an interesting side story concerning this place, because back about 1910 a prospector purchased this land and had high hopes that it would produce the mother lode. When that dream fell apart this man despaired to the point that he committed suicide by diving headfirst into a barrel of water.

CHAPTER SIX

NEW ADVENTURES

D uring the long winter nights in the late 60s, Clara and Hap worked on the concept of a new type of fishhook. Convinced that there had to be a better way of catching fish than tearing their mouths apart and then losing them, Hap came up with a different idea. After much trial and error he devised a hook with the end of the barb on a sphere. This barb rotated and slipped into the cross position when taken by a fish.

Bowden hinged hook, 20,000 hooks manufactured, 1976-78.

This hook was patented in Canada, the US and Japan, and after years of negotiation, 20,000 hooks were manufactured in Hong Kong by a man named Luke who visited the Bowdens during the 70s. This involved an enormous outlay of capital, as Hap hints that it ate up the best part of their bankroll. Just a short time after the hooks were marketed the barb ban came into law. Further, there was a downside in that once the barb turned sideways it could not be extracted and therefore had to be run on through the sides of the fishes' mouths. No matter, though, even if it wasn't a huge success, it was a challenge that they were prepared to face and it certainly didn't discourage these people from trying; they just moved on to other adventures.

The restless nature of the Bowdens again reared its head in 1977. After many years of guiding and ranching they sold the whole lot to their sons, sold their airplane and headed west to the ocean. It was time for new excitement and adventure. They took a good long look at the fishing industry and purchased a commercial fishing licence for $100,000. Next they bought a boat for $150,000. Called *Pacific Wind*, it was to be their home for the next three years.

The *Pacific Wind*, 1979.

The downside of this venture was undoubtedly the weather, as they frequently had to take refuge from terrible storms. They recalled the time that they went out on a six-knot forecast and ran into eighteen-knot winds. Someone complained over the radio about the poor performance of the weather bureau whereupon the weatherman came on air and said, "I don't make the weather, I just report it."

One of Clara's most powerful memories of the fishing years was the time at Ucluelet where they stopped to get fuel. As she walked along the dock, she slipped and fell into the ocean. Somehow a wave threw her right back onto the dock again. It happened so fast she could hardly believe it. Only the fact that she was soaked proved it had happened. The next day the attendant, who had noticed the incident, asked, "Are you going to do a morning dip for us again today?"

Fishing was, at times, an exercise in frustration: such as the shaft trouble that they had a terrible time rectifying. By the time they got it fixed they had lost three weeks of the best fishing period.

Some notes from Clara's diary include, "Put new Loran on *Pacific Wind*." "Got radiophone." "Got 50 hake so we're having hake for supper."

On July 7th she wrote, "It is really rough. Baked apple pie for supper but I'm not hungry."

The next day she wrote, "Lost our anchor; we're on our way to Ucluelet to get another anchor and fuel."

On the 12th she wrote, "We got 174 fish; best ever. We ran the power plant all night to freeze them."

A week later they stopped at Ucluelet again and went to visit two friends named Victor Ericson and Ole Olson, who had mined along the Quesnel River in the 40s and 50s. When they got to Ollie's place, he was pleasantly surprised to see them and told them that he would call Victor who lived in the adjacent cabin. Then Ole went to the sink and hollered to Victor who answered a moment later and then came to the cabin to visit. Clara told me that they got the greatest kick out of this unique telephone system that the two men had developed.

Clara filleting fish, 1978.

Somehow they had found out that the pipes were connected and that the sound traveled through them much like a telephone. They didn't have to go outdoors to communicate.

When they got back out to sea, Clara learned the joy of being on the ocean. That night her diary entry was brief to say the least, "Up-chucked; no supper; rough."

A week later she wrote, "The tap seized on the oil stove; we cooked supper over a propane torch."

Although they loved the freedom and adventure of life on the ocean, their free spirits decried the bureaucracy involved. Fishery officers constantly hounded them, checked their hold and found the tiniest reason to complain. The breaking point finally arrived when the officers boarded the vessel and found them with many filleted fish. The Bowdens were informed that they had to go to school for three days to learn how to fillet fish. That broke it. They both decided it was time to return to the wilderness. They sold the licence and the vessel at a loss of over $20,000, but considered it worth the loss to be rid of the bureaucracy they have always detested so completely.

Hap at work on the fish boat, 1978.

Once rid of the boat, the Bowdens headed to Victoria where they got permission to build a dwelling on their new mineral claim five miles up the Quesnel River from Beaver-mouth. Permission was granted with the condition that no stone, concrete or anything of a permanent nature was used in construction. There was also a size limitation on the dwelling that would come back to bite them later.

Just prior to their commercial fishing venture, Clara and Hap had sold a claim for $5,000. A short time later the price of gold skyrocketed and the claim increased dramatically in value. The buyer of said claim now has it for sale, along with several other claims, for an asking price of $1 million. Hap confesses that no one told him that gold prices were going to go through the roof, for if they had he never would have sold that claim. As for some of the other claims and how well they had done with them, Hap joked that he would tell me if I promised to keep quiet. I agreed, but when I asked how they made out on the other claims, Hap replied, "You're not keeping quiet."

It seems that the Bowden humour even rubbed off on their children. I'm thinking of the time Ab got a coyote and decided to have a little fun with his dad. He jammed the coyote in between two trees and then told his dad that it had committed suicide. Hap swears that he didn't buy it for one second.

Always ready for new adventure, the Bowdens arrived back in Quesnel. The year was 1981, and they had a plan: they were going to get rich in the prospecting field. They worked their claim along the Quesnel River, which was extremely hard work, but they had their independence and managed to make a decent living at the same time. They would start work at four in the morning and quit at ten.

Coyote jammed between trees.

This allowed them to beat the heat of the day and still have time to build up the new Bowdenville that was soon to appear.

Hap and Clara's sluicebox in action.

When they took breaks from mining, they set about building their new home as well as a host of other buildings. Hap bought a Skidoo and then built a riverboat for working the waterway, while Clara was busy at a million projects. Her diary notes that she made carrot wine and ginger beer. Another example of Clara's ability to make use of everything was displayed when their pup tore up a life jacket. In no time flat Clara had turned the remains of the jacket into some cushions.

Hard at work prospecting, they had reached bedrock by March 1983 where they picked up one nice nugget in black sand and found fair-sized colours to boot. Their prospecting venture was becoming more interesting by the day.

Throughout the summer of 83, outbuildings began appearing at Bowdenville. A large garden with a variety of trees had taken shape;

as well they had chickens, turkeys and bees to supplement their diet and afford them the independence that seems as necessary to them as life itself.

The correspondence that traveled back and forth between the Bowdens and government offices was huge. I'm certainly glad that I was not one of the officials that had to deal with them. According to Hap, he got permission from Victoria to build a cabin on their claim, providing no cement or bricks were used. In other words, it was to be a temporary dwelling. But when a representative from Lands came to check, a good-sized building had been erected. More than just a bit shocked, the visitor shouted, "This is illegal; the building can't be more than 12 feet."

Clara says that she doesn't know what inspired her, but she blurted out, "That's all there is; 12 feet for me and 12 feet for Hap."

The gentleman left and the next time he returned was in response to a request from the Bowdens to purchase a piece of land. As soon as he entered the room Hap got up and left. Alone with Clara, the man asked, "Don't you have something to say about this?"

Clara came back with, "I don't see why it hurts for us to have a little piece of land out here." This forced the man to ask her to come outside where he stomped his foot, pointed to the ground and said, "The peg goes right there."

Well, it turned out that the new Bowdenville was about to take place with room to spare because they would eventually end up with eight acres.

During the winter of 83/84 Hap found time to build a magnificent wagon. An enormous amount of labour went into this endeavor but the end result was worthwhile. It was all made of birch and was a piece of art to say the least. This wagon even made its way into a parade.

Hap's wagon.

One of the pastimes in the Bowden household was a pool table that they often put to good use. It must have been a piece of cake for Hap to win at the table, that is until April when Clara noted in

123

her diary, "I beat Hap in a game of pool, believe it or not."

Though they were in the wilderness so to speak, that didn't stop Clara and Hap from making improvements that one would expect in contemporary city life. For instance, it didn't take long for them to install a pipeline and have running water in their new home. This was just one of many remarkable improvements that were made over the next few years as we shall see.

During the spring of 84 some of the gold finds on successive days were: 17 grains, 23 grains, 29 and 22 grains. This was recovered during four-hour shoveling sessions. A week later they recovered 59 and 58 grains on successive days. This was definitely paying the rent. Soon they purchased a tractor and bucket in order to make things easier.

Clara was forever making clothing for someone. If it is true that idleness is the workshop of the devil, then it must follow that Clara's hands worked for another source because they were always making things for others. In June she made a complete cowgirl outfit for her granddaughter Reanna, who was becoming a riding sensation in the Quesnel area.

In September even more gold was obtained. During three successive days they brought up 85, 57 and 115 grains. Hap informed me that they often made between $50 and $150 per day.

Clara noted that she had planted apricot, lilacs, currants, gooseberries, many different types of herbs and 98 strawberry plants. She also found time to make rosehip wine. She further noted that Al, the gold buyer, had arrived at their claim. No mention was made of the value of gold that was sold. A silent bunch, these gold miners, wouldn't you say?

During August and September all spare time was spent building a garage and power plant shed. In addition, there was a steady stream of visitors to Bowdenville. Surely Clara and Hap would be millionaires if they had been paid for all the free meals they supplied throughout the years.

In October, aside from testing new locations for gold, Hap got a bear that was rendered down and from which they managed to obtain one gallon of oil. This is just a small idea of the way in which these people lived off the land.

Three claims were registered in November at a cost of $210. These claims were right in the area of their home.

Always inventive, Clara gathered willows and weaved some baskets, then filled them with moss and pinecones, sprayed silver paint on them and made decorative hanging baskets. Their home was and is a testimony to their ingenious natures. Almost everything on the place is homemade or taken from nature.

With the arrival of winter it was back to Sundberg's where they cut new trails and spent a month trapping. In her spare time Clara kept her knitting needles warm by always creating something or other.

During early 1986 many days were spent widening the right-of-way into their property so that the sun could dry out the roadway. As well they pur-

Hough loader and hopper, c1985.

chased a Hough loader, set up a monitor and got down to some serious prospecting. After fixing some minor problems with the monitor, they ran 140 yards through and came out with $900 for one and a half days' labour. It didn't take long for them to realize that the hopper was too short causing a loss of gold. This was just one of a series of problems that hounded them incessantly. But they certainly had

Clara displays two and a half ounces of gold taken in three days' cleanup. 1985.

their good days. Clara's diary noted, "Got to work at 7:45, quit at 6:00. Put through sixty-seven loads today. Got over two ounces of gold or roughly $700."

Also during the summer of 86 son Brad and his wife Lori built a new house and barn at Sundberg's. This once wilderness area was being transformed into an easily accessible hunting camp that was a far cry from the days when Clara and Hap first took pack trains into the area.

It was in 87 that Clara got a Maytag washer. Was it as good as the ads say? Clara states that as best she can remember it worked very well. Next on the order list was a propane power plant. Power was so necessary to their future plans, such as building an airplane. In March they traded their Hough loader for some property in Wells. Then it was off to the trap line at Sundberg and Chiaz Lakes.

April fourth found them staking another claim known as Lehna's claim. No sooner had they finished, then two men came along intent on staking the same ground. This ground seemed to produce better results because Clara took note that they worked four hours, made a good haul and then boiled coffee over an open fire. Always open to a deal, they bought a Flying Dutchman sluice box from a fellow named Chuck Sorenson and paid for it in gold. She also took note that Hap shot a huge black bear right in their garden. Such is the reality of living in remote areas.

Some quotes from Clara's diary are brief but the message is clear. Such as the entry for July 6th that reads, "Hit bedrock and hit the jackpot so we cleaned up and left." Once again I would have preferred a dollar amount. Another entry read, "Hap was almost hit by a rolling boulder today." This sort of thing was a constant threat to these miners, as well as slides and cave-ins that took a great many lives.

The August 10, 1987 entry took note that they had cleaned the sluice box and got 273 grains. At 480 grains to an

Hap with Flying Dutchman sluice box, 1985.

ounce, they obviously had a good day. At times they took grandson Mitch along on their sluicing ventures and gave him a split of the take when they cleaned up. This certainly must have given the young lad a thing called excitement.

Forever wheeling and dealing, Hap and Clara sold the recently acquired land at Wells for a Ford 4-wheel drive as down payment and a house trailer was thrown in as part of the deal. Hap claims that they didn't make any money on this venture but they had the excitement of wheeling and dealing and that can certainly make life interesting.

October found them back in the Edwards Lake area, cutting trail in preparation for trapping season. I also must point out that Clara ran her own trap line. No sissy here. During the long winter nights Clara spent much of her time sewing or knitting, such as the entire day she spent making a skating skirt and top for granddaughter Reanna. Her work was rewarded, though, because Reanna won a gold medal.

During December Hap took a trip to their claim only to find that vandals had struck. The lean-to and table they had constructed were smashed beyond repair. Everything had been ransacked and destroyed. Clara clearly made the point that Hap was devastated when he arrived home. It didn't take him long to drown his sorrow, though, and he did it by immersing himself in his favorite pastime–building furniture.

It was May 1988 that a complement of batteries arrived to augment the solar panels they had installed. A powerhouse was constructed and the 20 batteries were installed. A steady supply of power was now available without using the propane power plant. Hap jokes that he actually put up two of these solar platforms but there wasn't enough sun for two so he had to take one down.

When spring arrived it was back to their claim where they worked for a few hours and made $40. Throughout all this time Clara's diary notes an endless parade of visitors. Surely there is something intriguing about people that try to live close to nature. It seems to attract people in droves.

The next order of business was to extend the size of the airplane hanger in preparation for their next airplane, and then Hap put on a pair of spurs and climbed a tree where he installed a wind direction indicator known as a wind sock.

Another oddity that must be mentioned was their dog, named

Hap putting up a wind sock at the age of 66, 1988.

Sparky. This was a rather unusual dog in that it thought it was a cat and was always trying to climb trees. There was one particular squirrel that used to come down out of the trees and tease Sparky relentlessly. She would get frustrated to the point where she would take a flying run and climb the trees just as high as possible in an attempt to get this squirrel. One day while the squirrel was teasing Sparky it lost its hold on a branch and tumbled to the ground. Like a flash Sparky went at it with the result that the squirrel escaped by a matter of inches only. Clara assured me that the squirrel used greater care after that.

One of the biggest problems faced by the Bowdens was finding someone to care for their place when they had to leave. Many times they let people stay free of charge in the adjacent cabin just to have someone around to watch the place when they were gone.

Finally in May, Hap and Clara drove to Vancouver where they put a down payment on an airplane. On their return they set about cutting trees along the roadway in order to widen it into an emergency airstrip. This was a major undertaking for two people of their age but it didn't faze them. Perhaps no one has told these people that they are getting up in years because they remain more active than most people half their ages.

When September rolled around Hap went guiding for son Brad. At the age of 66 he surely must have found the mountains a lot higher and steeper than when he was 30 or 40 years of age. When he returned from guiding, the airplane, an Avid amphibian, had arrived. They dismantled it and put it in the hangar for painting, then began the tedious job of riveting and putting an extension on the wings. By October the plane was ready for its first inspection, which it passed with flying colours. Not too bad for two elderly bush rats.

The Avid amphibian airplane, 1990.

I asked Hap if Clara ever got her pilot's licence and always the comedian he replied, "No! Women weren't meant to fly; if they were we would call it a box office instead of a cockpit."

Oh, pardon me while I groan.

The month of December arrived to find Hap and Clara back on the trap line. They were cutting trail into ever more remote areas and enjoying every minute of it. They were shocked to find that some of their previous trails were overgrown and stacked with down-trees. Hap sure hit it right when he pointed out that nothing stands still in nature. Just neglect your trails for a while and they will soon disappear.

Clara wrote, "We headed to the trap line early, baited Crooked Lake lines and then on to Tiny Creek and Amanda Lake. When we got home our dog Sparky was missing. We called and she howled so we searched and found her in a trap on Ling Creek. When we released her she headed for home. No harm done but she knows what a trap is now."

Back from trapping, they went to work assembling the plane with great vigor. Clara wrote in her diary, "Lots of work putting ribs together – gluing, fibreglassing and painting. Fit a sponson on the plane and worked on the landing gear. Drilled 59 holes on axle covering. Riveted sponsons on and then glued and put foam on them. Cut ceconite cloth for wings and had to put a French seam in them."

This was just an example of what Clara's diary looked like during that winter. On April 10th the plane was rolled out and the wings were installed. By the 24th they had put the fabric on the rudder, stabilizer and elevators, plus cloth on the wings. When they finished putting the windshield on the plane Clara wrote, "What a job putting it in on a curve." A week later Hap passed his medical and was getting ready for flight.

One of their greatest successes, from my point of view, was the many grapes that they planted in their new greenhouse. While visiting them I tried the grapes and they were delicious. They also make first class wine. I was surprised to find grapes growing so profusely in that climate. What a difference a bit of TLC can make. As well Clara noted, "Picked five gallons of strawberries for wine. We will distill it into brandy."

After what must have seemed an interminable time Clara wrote, "Finally put the last window in our plane and riveted the front seat down. Put the wings on, folded them back and loaded the plane on a trailer so we can take it to town for painting."

One rather unusual event took place in early November when Hap got to reminiscing about his youth when he used to work out on the athletic rings. Convinced that he could still do anything he used to do, he set up the rings and started working out. Everything went all right until he tried a rather tricky dismount that he had perfected many years earlier; then disaster struck. Clara recalls, "I had just put bread in the oven when Hap staggered into the house with one arm completely separated from the socket. I took him to town and Dr. Sears put it back in place and gave him some pain pills. Hap sure put in a rough night."

It was back to guiding and trapping again in late 89, where Clara spent the evenings knitting an Afghan for Brad's wife; Lori. Meanwhile Hap brought in the New Year by buying granddaughter Reanna a violin and paying for her lessons.

Their efforts to get the plane operational were constantly met with frustration, such as the four months they had already spent waiting for an engine to be shipped from Texas. One excuse followed another when they were told that the engine had to be test run for another 40 hours. A week later they were informed that another 60 hours had to be put on the engine. This nonsense continued until April when they phoned and learned that the engine was experiencing carburetor trouble. Fed up, Hap and Clara demanded their money back and ordered a new engine. By the time June rolled around they had fitted the new engine only to find out that it turned the prop the wrong way. They returned the engine for a swap only to find out that they didn't make the other kind. Again they took a loss when the company only returned $150. The costs kept escalating as they found out when they had to pay $350 US just for the gauges.

Always looking for new mountains to climb, Hap spent some time building different kinds of snowshoes. For every idea he tried there was a downside. Some iced up too much while others worked fine on the flats but were slippery on the slopes. He finally realized that a lot of engineering had already gone into the development of snowshoes.

All throughout the summer they worked on the airplane and still found the spare time to construct a cement root cellar. They had an endless amount of problems finding the right parts or waiting for supplies for the airplane. Finally on July 15th Clara wrote, "Did the last five cam locks to join cowling, cut out side windows, set up ailerons and flaps, then adjusted the control system and started to run in the motor." The next day she added, "Put in the last side window and did the weight and balance check. Loaded the plane on the trailer and took it to the airport parking lot. Inspector Larry Allen of Transport Canada passed the plane."

Several more problems surfaced during taxiing tests, such as overheating, but the worst occurred when the locking pin gave on the under carriage and the wingtips and bottom of the plane were scratched. It was back for repairs until August 2nd when Hap got the plane airborne. It flew well but when he landed the rivets pulled out of the right side of the axle. Again it was back to the repair shop until August 10th when Hap again took it up for a flight. As he was merrily cruising along the engine seized up. He notified the control tower that he had lost his engine and was attempting an emergency landing in a farmer's field. Fortunately, Hap was near a farmer's field at 1000 feet when the mishap occurred so he managed to make a safe landing.

As he came in, a mare and colt were right in his flight path and he cleared them by about ten feet. When he got the plane stopped he noticed that the two horses were on the opposite side of the field. They obviously had set a record pace crossing the field.

I asked Hap, "Was it a rough landing?"

"A little bit." He replied.

Once down, the plane was loaded back on the trailer and taken back to their home, where the wings were removed and the craft placed in the hangar. At once Hap and Clara started sending out inquiries to see if anyone wanted to purchase it. Understandably they had endured enough. When Hap went to collect on the faulty engine he received word that there was no warranty and that he was supposed to stay within gliding distance of an airport. The problem with the engine was discovered and it turned out to be a vapor lock in the oil pump. By some miracle it seems that the engine ran for four hours without any oil.

This airplane venture did not turn out to be a moneymaker, as the plane cost them $25,000 plus a great amount of work. A year later they sold it for $22,000.

Searching for new horizons, Hap set to work building his own 12-volt deep freeze. He used one-quarter inch plywood on the inside. Then two inches of foam, a layer of tinfoil and then one inch of foam, another layer of tinfoil and then two inches of foam. This was sealed in with another layer of plywood. Did it work, you ask? You bet. In fact it is still working well and runs off a combination of power from the Pelton wheel, which runs off waterpower, and the solar panels. There was a price to pay for this equipment, though, for just a week later they had to purchase three new batteries for the solar panel at a cost of $1419.

One highlight from Clara's diary includes the day her son Ab came upriver with his jet boat. He took them for a ride up to 20-mile and Quesnel Forks. Clara noted that it was a beautiful day and a beautiful trip.

When late fall came around it was back to the trap line for Clara, while Hap returned to the guiding business to assist Brad. At 68 years Hap was still taking out hunters. Surely he must have found it tough to keep up with the younger men.

An opportunity offered itself for Clara and Hap in December when they purchased the Joe Reid Lease for $250. This was a ten-year tenure and a chance to get some high potential diggings. Clara noted that they paid $25 for a free miner's licence but added that it would only be $1 next year, obviously because she would be 65 years of age then.

When January 1991 arrived the Bowdens were back trapping. When they took their fur to the sale they averaged $53.67 for each marten. When one considers that they sometimes got five martens in a day, it becomes apparent that we are talking real money here. Although they were slowing up a bit on the trapping, they were not bored because they had the never-ending job of getting up firewood and many trips into Quesnel to watch their grandson Mitch play hockey. Seemingly inspired by their presence, Mitch would often make their day by scoring a goal or two.

A new interest came into Clara's life when she got a guitar and starting spending some time practicing chords. A few weeks later she noted that the tips of her fingers were hardening and she could start to hear what the chords should sound like.

The next item on the agenda was the purchase of a one and a half inch pump for mining. Clara wrote, "We moved the sluice box and got some nice gold." For a change of pace, they walked a couple miles upriver to where a huge slide had come down. It had raced down from the banks across the river, but with such force that the material was piled up high on the opposite bank of the river with many of the trees still standing upright. Apparently the slide had actually blocked the river for a time before the snow was gone.

Prospector Ben Miller, who lives on the riverbank several miles below the slide, got a first-hand view of the power of nature. When the dammed-up slide let go he heard an enormous roar as the earth, with the trees tumbling end over end, came roaring by his house.

Ben is an experienced woodsman, having spent over fifty years prospecting and trapping the Quesnel River country. A veteran who was in the infantry during World War Two, Ben has many interesting stories about his years in the mountains.

Clara got a scare in June that she noted in her diary, "I was watering the hanging baskets on the front porch when I must have had a dizzy spell. I fell against the pick-up and to the ground and split my upper lip in half. I wasn't dizzy, I just blacked out somehow." Although the lip was badly swollen the next day, she didn't bother going for medical aid. A short time later she experienced heart trouble

Trapper and prospectorBen Miller picture, circa 1955.

and had to wear a monitor for a while. Whatever the problem was it seems to have disappeared because she is still a tiger that is up a five in the morning, often getting a load of firewood before breakfast.

To make their transition to wilderness independence complete, Hap and Clara purchased a stone grinder so they could grind wheat and make their own flour. Then it was back to town to get some tobacco plants. These people were intending to become self-sufficient. As they were always looking for more electric power, a wind charger was placed on the rooftop and at times added to the grid. Once again Hap joked that he actually put up two chargers but there wasn't enough wind for two so he had to take one down.

Often Clara made notes of their daily affairs, such as the entry that read, "Made $37 in gold today in one hour." Or, "Hap put up a drying rack over the stove today. I'm drying green peppers and cucumbers."

October found Hap and Clara on their way back to Sundberg's for another trapping session. They got a deer on the way and had to lose a day by bringing it home. Back on the line Clara noted several days' take of fur, "Five marten, seven marten, five marten and six marten." Not a bad few days' pay at $50 to $60 each.

Shortly after they built their house at Bowdenville, Hap and Clara constructed a fine cabin. This forced me to ask, "Why did you go to all the work of building a cabin when you already had a house?"

Hap looked at me as if he felt sorry for me and explained, "What if the house burned down in the middle of the winter? We would freeze to death!" Did I mention that these people are practical?

Since the chance of break-in or vandalism was such a worry, they moved a man named Tom Crawford into the cabin so there would be someone around in their absence. Then they set to work building a large woodshed at the cabin and supplied a large amount of firewood for their guest. It has always intrigued me that the Bowdens see fit to get up wood for their guests even though their guests are much younger than they are. Perhaps they realize that many of us spend a good portion of our lives in the cities and therefore require more tender care.

When January 92 rolled around Hap was busy compassing and staking another claim, known as Dale White's Claim. Also, they spent many days getting firewood for Tom's cabin. It was a rare day, in fact probably about once a year, that Clara wrote, "I didn't do a thing today."

One day while splitting firewood Hap sent a block flying from his axe right into Clara's ankle. She hobbled around for a while but again she did not go for medical aid. While I'm on the subject of firewood, I must mention an invention that impressed me a great deal. It is a used truck tire that Hap put on top of their wood-splitting block. When they split a block into pieces, the pieces stay within the tire so they do not have to continually bend over and pick up each piece as most wood-splitters do. Did I mention that these people are inventive?

When son Brad and his wife Lori went to a sports' show, Clara stayed with their children, Mitch, Reanna and Riley who was taking violin lessons at the time. I understand that Riley really enjoyed playing for her grandparents. Did Clara just take it easy while tending the children? Not a chance; she put her

Hap's tire stops wood from falling off chopping block after it is split.

knitting needles to work and continued making presents for others.

During February their guest, Tom, got sick and had to go to the hospital. During his absence Clara completely cleaned the cabin and porch, including the deep freeze. Washed all his clothes, sheets and pillowcases, and even made him a new set of pillowcases. And then as if she hadn't done enough, she repaired a zipper in one of his coats. Trust me when I state that these people are energetic.

It was in late March when Hap, Clara and Mitch went for a walk upriver on the crusted snow. They found where a slide had came down and noticed a house log in the debris. At once it became apparent that a cabin had been destroyed. As they moved along they came upon a four-point deer that had been killed by the wolves. It would have been a perfect day except that Clara dropped through the crusted snow and landed on some object severely damaging her ribs. She suffered for several weeks, but she did not seek medical attention.

Although it may sound unbelievable, it was at this point that Clara and Hap filed application forms to buy the property they were on. This forces me to wonder how the authorities could have denied them when they already had a good-sized community in progress.

Never one to be stumped by a problem, Clara related how she made a pair of slippers and found that somehow she had made one smaller than the other. She solved the problem by making another copy of each and so ended up with two pairs. She also mentioned a trip they made to town to see granddaughter Alena's medals and cup that she won skiing. The pride Clara felt for the many accomplishments of her grand kids plainly comes through in her writings.

Now that they had someone to tend the place while they were away, Hap and Clara bought a camper and set off to the Yukon. Clara noted that they fished in Teslin Lake and that Hap had caught a large lake trout that they roasted over an open campfire. Then it was on to Robert Service's cabin in Dawson where they heard Tom Burns recite many of those famous poems. The next stop mentioned was at Duncan Springs where Hap traded many of his fishhooks for ivory recovered from mastodons.

Another stop was made at Fort McPherson where they took pictures of the Lost Patrol's graveyard. These men ate their own dogs and finally perished only 20 miles from the Fort after 50 days on the trail. On their way home, Clara and Hap stopped for a photo shoot at Arctic Circle.

After their return home, Clara and Hap went to their old ranch for

Hap and Clara at Arctic Circle, 1992.

a load of sawdust. It is clear from Clara's writing that a great wave of nostalgia overcame them as they realized that 30 years had passed since they made that sawdust.

All through the years, former hunters returned to visit the Bowdens and reminisce. Sometimes these gab sessions would turn into near all night sessions. One such visitor was the man who had taken the record grizzly bear many years earlier.

An odd entry in Clara's diary noted the time she made rosehip wine with disastrous results. She wrote, "I woke up this morning to find that the wine had blown its lid. It came through the upper floor and ran all over the barrel stove. I put only half as much water as I should have and way too much yeast." Clara sure didn't give up, though, she went out and picked another batch of rosehips and made six gallons of wine. Then it was back to the trap line where they set some personal records by catching seven, eight and ten martens on different days during their stay in the woods. Sometimes Mitch would accompany them on the trap line, and he was always rewarded for any furs he caught. Clara often went to great lengths to prepare good food out in the mountains. In fact, some of the descriptions of meals she prepared simply make my mouth water. Speaking from experience I can honestly say that the finished product is even better than the descriptions.

The Bowdens display a fine catch of martens. Also in the photo are a home-made chair and deep freeze, 1992.

Christmas brought a special surprise when they received aluminum snowshoes from their sons' families, and New Years Day 1993 was celebrated in style when their sons' families came out and a lively party ensued. Clara wrote, "Bob James came by with his guitar and Riley played the violin. We had a great time out there in the woods. Sparky [their dog] got into Howey's vodka and got drunk; he is really sick."

Clara's description of their windmill on the roof seemed rather odd. When Mitch stayed over with them, he slept upstairs and a big storm hit. Apparently the sound of the windmill really rocked him to sleep. I questioned Hap as to why the windmill no longer graced their rooftop and he told me that during a particularly bad storm the windmill almost brought the house down and that led to its disappearance.

At times Clara and Hap broke the isolation by going to watch their grand kids ski. Such as the February trip to Troll Resort where Alena, Carrie and Jesse performed for them. *The Cariboo Observer* is replete with stories of their successes on the slopes.

One of the things that surprised me the most was when I was shown two coffins that Clara and Hap had made. They finished them in April when, as Clara wrote, "Hap finished putting the handles on the coffins; they're good and strong now. I put Thompson water seal on them. They look good."

Recently when I phoned and asked Hap how he was doing, he

replied, "Well I'm still looking down instead of up."

Forever in search of adventure, Clara and Hap went with their two sons on a jet boat trip up the Tuchodi River to the lake in Northern BC. This is a scenic and potentially dangerous trip but they made it, and son Ab got a six-point elk that he proudly displays to this day. Clara summed up the trip by briefly stating, "We had a beautiful and scenic trip."

The down side of the Tuchodi trip was that water got under the Teflon coating on the bottom of the boat and lifted it thereby destroying its usefulness. After they returned home Hap spent two month's working on the boat to restore it. All of the Teflon had to be taken off and the 480 bolts that had supported the Teflon, had to be removed and the holes welded.

Clara's gardens and greenhouse which was used for growing grapes, tomatoes and cucumbers, 1993.

Clara has proved that one can grow watermelon in the Quesnel area. During the summer of 1990 she grew some excellent fruit, watermelons among them. Also, her idea of planting grapes in her greenhouse has born fruit, if you'll pardon the pun. Just last October I saw the clusters hanging and waiting for picking.

In late September she wrote, "I picked the last of the grapes and made five gallons of wine." She also noted a first, "Today I ran our washing machine on solar and water power [Pelton wheel] and it runs good." As they were always searching for more power, a simple solution came to mind. They moved the power shed with the Pelton wheel further down the hill. This increased the water drop by 40 feet and created a considerable increase in power.

Forever searching for new experiences, Hap purchased a fly-tying outfit and began making his own flies. Just a short time later he bought a band saw to aid in his furniture-making hobby. His first two projects were a cradle and a hope chest for Reanna. Just recently he gave me a beautiful lawn chair with the old Bowden Ranch brand stamped into it. I will treasure it always.

A strange event took place in August 1994 when their new tenant, Howey Meeker, poisoned himself. It seems that he drank devil's club tea without first taking the barbs off the plant. Clara noted that he got extremely ill and had to be taken to the doctor who prescribed something for him. The effect was a leg that was all red and swollen.

The next day Clara noted, "Howey's leg is swollen from the foot to the knee. It's spreading and getting worse." And again a few days later, "Howey went to town to get penicillin; he has to go into the hospital." A week later he finally returned home with the infection under control.

When late October rolled around it was back to the trapline where they got some big beavers. While Clara was busing in the cookhouse, Hap called on the CB that he had a deer and needed her to help bring it in. Meanwhile grandson Jesse managed to get his first deer at the age of 12. I assume he was a rather proud lad to say the least.

It was in March 95 that cougar trouble started to present itself. Their tracks were spotted near the house about the same time that the Bowdens noticed their two house cats were missing. This was just a hint of more trouble to follow.

The situation with the purchase of their land finally came to fruition when a man from Lands came and they had it out. Clara noted, "Surveyors from Lands at Williams Lake came and we had it out. They argued about the location of the Initial Post. They resurveyed and then had lunch. At last it's over, I hope." It was. They ended up with eight acres and were more than pleased with the end result.

CHAPTER SEVEN
THE GOLDEN YEARS

After so many years of doing virtually everything imaginable one would surely think it was time for the Bowdens to retire to a life of leisure, but not a chance. Instead they tackled what was perhaps the toughest challenge of their lives. In April 95 they headed for Chilliwack, BC. Their destination was the Murphy Aircraft Co. that supplied airplane kits. They put a down payment on a Super Rebel 2500 and then headed back home. This was a good-sized airplane with the same sized wings as a Beaver – the workhorse of the North. Clara and Hap both agree that they never realized the astounding amount of work they had put themselves in for.

Back home they bought a small sawmill and began cutting lumber for the large workshop and hanger they would need to construct and store the craft. They also applied for Forest Service permission to cut trees along the proposed emergency airstrip, which was along the roadway. The approval was granted, but with the condition that the timber would go to salvage as they had priority.

Totally absorbed in the preparation work for the arrival of the plane kit, Clara and Hap began to notice that their TV reception was going from bad to worse. They investigated and found that a large bee's nest had been built across the receiver with a spout hanging down. Strange things happen out in the forest. And then, as if there wasn't enough activity around the place they even got some pigeons, supposedly as company for the turkeys and chickens.

It was back to Chilliwack in October where they received instructions on how to assemble the plane. The Super Rebel must have been quite popular because there were 16 other people taking the course. While there, they assembled a wing and all attending were taken up for a flight in one of these airplanes. Back home Hap went and helped a friend with the same kit and he got some valuable instructions on putting the wings together. Then they set to building the many tables necessary to construct the wings.

One of the bright sides of living far from civilization was that they were constantly visited by wildlife. Among the visitors were wolves, coyotes, bears, moose, deer, foxes and cougars. Also there were the countless hummingbirds that dropped by to gorge themselves at the feeder. Both Clara and Hap feel that their association with wildlife was the most important part of their wilderness experiences.

Some notes included in Clara's diary for February 96 include, "… We sent $2500 US to Murphys for the tail section of the Super Rebel….I melted down two frames of honey and got three kg of liquid honey…I finally finished the green and pink slippers; it takes over four hours for each of them."

Solar panels tower over Bowdenville.

There was a rather frantic entry by Clara on June 28th, "Hap came in about 2:30. He cut three fingers while he was working with the table saw; one of them was cut off and another was just hanging. I drove him to emergency at the hospital. He has to fly to Vancouver as there is no one in Prince George who can help him. He has to go to Dr. Grober in Vancouver." The next day she added, "Hap phoned. He had his fingers pinned and a cast put on. He hasn't eaten since he left so he's pretty weak."

Hap's operation was by no means a success. The reattached portion of the finger that was almost severed is dead and forever in the way. Hap sometimes says he may get that portion taken off again because it is just a nuisance.

As soon as Haps hand was well enough to work, it was back to falling trees on the emergency airstrip. This was a huge job that required moving the trees and fallen debris far enough to give clearance under the wings during takeoffs and landings. Clara's diary details the many days spent in this work and the dragging that was necessary to free the strip of loose rocks that could fly up and damage the aircraft on takeoff.

Then it was off to Chilliwack where they loaded the airplane kit on a trailer and transported it home. On November 16th they started work on the plane. Little did they realize that over five years would pass before the aircraft would take to the sky.

The ambition of these elderly people is almost passed belief. Just a few examples: they went back to Chilliwack to get the airplane wings; they built a garage for their guest cabin; they cut a good supply of firewood for the house, workshop and guest cabin; they went shopping for a rivet gun, drill press and many other tools; they finished the back spar assembly and it passed inspection, and in their spare time they did some prospecting and picked up some gold to help pay the bills.

By this time the work on the plane was going fairly well, except for the many phone calls to Chilliwack for clarification of details regarding the plane. Sometimes they put in a full day on the plane, riveting, deburring, dimpling and cromating. By July 19th they had finished the right wing and started on the left. Many times they were assisted in this work by grandkids Mitch and Jesse who must have been so proud of their grandparents for undertaking such a challenge at their ages.

Also assisting on the plane construction from time to time was a friend named Ron Harrison. In return Hap helped Ron stake several claims in the area. Ron and his wife Norma have recently settled in the area and their friendship with Clara and Hap has grown steadily during this time.

By September 18th the second wing was ready for inspection. Then it was back to Chilliwack for another load of plane parts. On

November 1st Clara wrote, "Started at 6 a.m. Worked on the flaps and ailerons and attached them to the wing. Came in around dark when Ab and Linda, Jesse and Riley surprised us at the back door. They had airplane books and a birthday cake for grandpa with a hunter and gun on top of the cake Linda made. We had a great 75th birthday for Hap; it was a nice visit."

December turned into a most frustrating time for Clara and Hap. In almost every shipment of supplies for the plane, parts were missing. This resulted in a fortune being spent on phone calls. The year 98 rolled around to find the airplane construction going big time. On January 22 Clara noted that they had worked ten hours on the plane.

The danger associated with life in the wilds was brought home with a bang on January 26th when Clara noted, "We woke up and Sparky was gone. Hap went up the hill to the water ponds and saw cougar tracks. He came back and said that the cougar probably got our dog. I checked the sheds and hanger but no response. As we walked by the front of our guest cabin we walked right into the cougar that had been just out of sight in the porch. It was eating on Sparky and it hissed at us from about ten feet. It could have been tragic if the cougar had not had enough room to escape over the woodpile as it would have been trapped and probably would have attacked us. Hap fired a quick shot and missed. It got away but a neighbor with a cougar hound came and we got it in 20 minutes." Did this make Clara and Hap consider moving closer to civilization?

Cougars can be a threat to pets.

Not a chance, they just added this experience to their endless collection of memories.

Clara has a rather strange entry for May, "Worked on plane and transplanted some plants to the garden, then I came in the house and found the floor flooded. I left the warm water tap on while getting my plants moved and forgot to shut it off, I guess. Hap and I each took a towel and mopped it all up. We now have the cleanest floor in the valley."

On June 8th Clara wrote, "We worked all day cromating the front of the plane. Riveted the corners and under the floor. Did some deburring as well. Now we're out of rivets." For a change of pace, they set up the Flying Dutchman sluice box on July 24, ran some gravel through, and then made 10 gallons of apricot wine. No use wasting part of the day.

Something that was long overdue was a Ward family reunion, so Clara was off to it in September. On her return she commented that they had held a barn dance and had a very nice time.

There are some disadvantages to living in remote areas as Clara and Hap again found out in October. A terrible storm had hit and left a mess in its wake. When they attempted to go to town they had to cut and remove 24 trees that had blown over and blocked the roadway. There's no question that life in the wilds is not for everyone. Perseverance is a must if one is to survive, as the thought of living in near isolation is something many people simply cannot handle. But according to Clara and Hap, they never had any problems with living in isolation and I suggest that one of the reasons for this was because they kept so active. They always had more plans on the drawing board than there were days in the year.

November 25th was truly a special day for the Bowden family because it marked their 50th wedding anniversary. A cake was brought to their home and a celebration was in order. When asked how they were holding up, Hap answered, "I'm afraid Clara is getting Alzheimer's because she can't seem to remember where I put things anymore."

Hap again demonstrated his ingenuity during the winter of 2000 when heavy snows fell on their garage. Rather than climb up to shovel off the roof with the inherent risks, Hap simply fired up his tiger torch inside the garage. Within a matter of minutes the roof heated up and the snow slid off. Did I mention that these people are clever?

Clara and Hap at their 50th wedding aniversary, 1999.

Their carefree existence was rudely interrupted in January, when Hap was diagnosed with prostate cancer. He went to Kelowna for a two-day exam and then returned home to wait. Finally on March 2nd he returned to Kelowna where he underwent treatment. At times he was terribly ill, but he hung in there and returned home over six weeks later. To this day he is still hanging in there, so it probably goes without saying that these people are also tough.

On one of my trips to Bowdens for an interview, I traveled with pilot Don Redden of Prince George. Don had already spent lots of time with Clara and Hap and had test-flown their new plane several times as well. But Don had a point to make about just how clever

147

Clara was, and he told me that he would prove it to me after we arrived at Bowdenville. Sure enough, while we were seated at the table Don asked, "Clara, will you bring one of the aircraft books because I want to check a certain thing?" He told her what part he was interested in and at once Clara grabbed one of the large books and opened it. She only had to flip a couple pages in that monster book and there was the part Don had referred to. Understandably I was more than a little impressed.

While many people are spending their final years in retirement homes, not so for the Bowdens. They continue to live at the end of a road 50 km from town. They still plant their large garden, grow clusters of grapes inside a greenhouse, pick wild berries, and cut their own firewood. The thought of moving near civilization is foreign to them and as Clara puts it, "We have to die somewhere, so why not here in a place we love?"

Clara and Hap continued working on the plane as the parts arrived; often they put in eight hours a day. Some of the prices shocked them, such as the tires and tubes that cost $1305. Clara noted, "Quite a price." At times their work was painfully frustrating, such as when the pictures didn't jive with the directions. In those cases it was back to the phone for some heated debates with the dealer.

Remains of main house after the fire, 1998.

On March 30th Ab and Linda checked the home ranch that they had sold and found it to be a terrible mess. A month later, in a deliberate act of arson, the ranch house and cabins were destroyed. This was heartbreaking news to Clara and Hap who realized that the efforts of so many years and the sum total of so many memories seemed to lie in the ashes of that despicable act.

There was always something of interest going on at Bowdenville. Such as the day a black bear started chasing their dog around the yard. Hap had to get the rifle to settle the dispute. Clara told me that they did a lot more around the place than just work on the plane. On August 28 she wrote, "Dug spuds in the new ground and got nine, five-gallon pails full. Canned five quarts of tomatoes and made seven quarts apple pie filling, then baked an apple pie. That's all for today."

Throughout the winter Clara noted that they were experiencing endless frustration with getting airplane parts and proper instructions. She wrote, "Putting the controls on the plane is really frustrating just trying to figure it out." They paid $2,000 for the instruments, and then, when the 265 HP Continental engine arrived in March it was short 26 bolts. Pure frustration was certainly not an overstatement.

The work on the plane was just one of countless chores and tasks they faced. For example, in September 2000 Clara wrote, "I picked two and a half gallons of Oregon grapes and made juice." And again, "I picked the last of the concord and white grapes and then made three batches of jelly." Another item in her diary shows that she was making four sets of slippers for Christmas presents. This was a constant for Hap and Clara. They were always making something for their grandchildren. It made me think that God, in his infinite mercy, sure got it right when he created grandparents.

Every couple weeks during the summer, they trudged up the hill to the water ponds that fed the Pelton wheel as well as their water supply. At least a gallon of bleach was used on each occasion to stop

Ab Bowden's family, left to right, Carrie, Jesse, Linda, Ab, and Alena, 2001.

the endless algae growth in the ponds. After each treatment, a certain amount of time was allowed for the bleach to work through the system before any water was used for drinking or cooking. Something I found a bit hilarious started in November 2000 when the Bowdens decided to go modern with a new satellite dish. The catch was that they had to install it themselves. Three full days were spent attempting to bring in the signal, but to no avail. With their patience exhausted Clara finally wrote, "Worked on the satellite dish again all day – no luck."

The next day she added, "Worked on the dish all day until 4 p.m. and then Hap had a brainwave. We stuck the s.o.b. on our old big dish and it worked. We got a 100 signal. Then we had to activate the programming and hurray! It came in bright and clear. Now we're playing with it to find out what each button does."

January 2001 started out with what could have been a terrible tragedy. Their grandson Jesse Bowden was with four of his friends at Groundhog Lake near Wells, BC, when he was buried in an avalanche. His friends set to work and after seven minutes found his helmet. Just a foot deeper they reached his head and managed to dig him out. Thankfully he was all right, and mercifully, the Bowdens did not find out about it until later so there was no worrying involved.

The next order of business was to put up a windsock on their emergency airstrip and this was a test for our pioneers. Clara noted, "We took some tools and went to hang the windsock. Our anchor tree bent a bit and we didn't make it. Should have more help."

The following day she added, "We did some repairing and hunting for more rope and lag screws etc., etc. Then we went down and hung the windsock. What a chore." And again the following day, "Kind of stiff. I've haven't been doing much of that kind of work, so I took it easy and went down to see if the windsock was flying. It's okay but kind of small."

All the hard work that had been involved in putting up the windsock went for naught, because a group of partiers came and tore it down, then left it on a picnic table at Beavermouth. Clara got the vehicle and licence plate numbers for the police but nothing ever came of it. The windsock was taken back to the airstrip and put up in another tree.

I must say I have a hard time trying to picture these people, Clara at 75 and Hap at 79 years of age, fooling around putting up windsocks. I

Clara and Hap with their Alaska sawmill, 2003.

suppose I shouldn't be surprised, though, because a year later they were still running their own sawmill.

As I previously mentioned, Clara and Hap had a pool table at the new Bowdenville, and Hap usually won the majority of games. But the February 17th entry in Clara's diary stated, "Boy, am I ever getting good at pool."

Perhaps Hap took offence at being handled in this manner and put in some steady practice, because five weeks later Clara noted, "I only beat Hap twice; he's getting too good."

It becomes obvious when interviewing Clara and Hap that they are satisfied with their lives and what they have accomplished. Certainly there can be no doubt that their work ethic has rubbed off on their sons who are both successful business people. Their grandchildren in turn seem to be cut from the same cloth and are well on their way to attaining their goals.

As for the Sundberg property, Brad still guides there although the place has changed much throughout the years. Access to the property is by vehicle, but the horses are still an integral part of Cariboo Mountain Outfitters.

As for the plane, after five and a half years, it finally took to the sky under the competent control of pilot Don Redden. Clara's November 9th diary entry reads, "Don Redden met us at the airport gate and tested it first. There were some problems with the brakes because of air in the lines. We fixed it and then went for a flight and it climbed

Brad Bowden's family. Left to right, Lori, Mitch, Riley, Reanna and Brad, 1996.

out like a homing pigeon at 1500 feet per minute and he didn't use full throttle."

Two weeks later with Hap on board Don flew the Super Rebel to Bowdenville where it was placed in the hanger for the winter.

The completed Super Rebel.

The total costs associated with the airplane are unknown, because many things were not included, such as all the assorted tools they purchased, and the Onan diesel power plant that was needed to power the tools associated with putting the plane together. A small fortune was spent on phone calls which were not included, and yet Clara's records totaled over $96,000 by the time the plane was finished. It took a total of 26,000 rivets and over 3,000 hours of labour to get this bird into the sky.

Just recently Don Redden and I returned to Bowdenville, where I interviewed Clara. At the same time, Don, Hap, and his friend Ron Harrison inspected the plane. Their mission was to find out why the plane had a tendency to roll slightly. If it is true that two heads are better than one, then it must also hold true that three heads are better than two. This was proven true in this case because within a few hours they had found the problem and knew how to rectify it. And so what does pilot Don Redden think of the finished product? He just returned from test-flying it since the renovations and he says the roll tendency was eliminated and it handles well. It has lots of power as well as short takeoff and landing capability. Its

Hap and Don Redden with the Super Rebel 2500 airplane, 2002.

stall speed is 38 MPH and this could be lowered even further with a few minor changes. All told he thinks they did a number one job of it. Once again the Bowdens have produced a winner.

Throughout the years the Bowdens have had several strange dogs, such as the one that climbed trees, but now they have yet another. Her name is Dolly and she is something to behold. Hap has a golf club that he keeps near the door just to entertain Dolly. He will bat a ball for a long distance and Dolly will faithfully retrieve it. Even though it often goes into the thick undergrowth at a considerable distance from the house, she will always find and return it. Does she get tired chasing this ball, you ask? You bet, and when she does, she takes a rest with the ball in her mouth just to make certain no one can throw it until she has recuperated. Then when she feels refreshed the game starts all over again. Just recently Don Redden and I took turns hitting the ball and watching Dolly retrieve it. At first she would run flat out to get the ball and run just as fast to bring it back to us. A couple of hours later she was so exhausted that she walked back with the ball a few times and then flopped on the ground. The game was over.

And so, it is always interesting to spend time at Bowdenville. There are few places that offer such an experience: such as sitting at the window and watching deer, or seeing three cougars walking along the road toward the house. I treasure the time I have spent with them and it is my sincere hope that I will visit with them for many years to come. There are so many memories they have to share that the hours simply fly by.

There are not many people left like Clara and Hap: people who put personal freedom above comfort and ease. When I recall the many things these people have done, I don't believe anything can show their practical nature with more clarity than the two caskets they have built for themselves. Hap picked out their favorite wood, pine for one and birch for the other, and built the caskets, and then Clara used her skill for the immaculate inner work. They have tried them out and state that they fit perfectly and are comfortable. As well, they have purchased two spots in the Quesnel Cemetery where they are to be laid to rest. Clara' grave marker will read:

Don't cry for me now; don't cry for me ever

For I will do nothing forever and ever.

Hap's grave marker will read:

Remember now as you pass by; as you are now so once was I.

As I am now you soon shall be; so now prepare to follow me.

This, ultimately, tells the story of their self-reliance and acceptance of nature and natural laws better than any other story of their most unusual lives.

The caskets are comfortable and fit perfectly.

In an effort to please Hap I want to include a few more of his favorite jokes at this point. The first one supposedly concerns a policeman who was a new arrival in the Quesnel area several years ago. On one of his first patrols, he was driving along when a cowboy

Clara and prospector Ben Miller, 2003.

passed him doing far over the posted speed limit. After a quick chase the cowboy was forced to pull his vehicle to the curb, at which point the policeman started writing out a ticket. He didn't have much luck, though, because a horsefly kept buzzing around his head. He slapped at it several times, to no avail, and then asked, "What is that thing anyway?"

"That's one of them circle flies," the cowboy replied, "they like to fly circles around a horse's ass all day long."

At that point the policeman stuck his head in the car window and asked, "Are you saying that you think I'm a horse's ass?"

"Oh no, officer, I don't think so," the cowboy answered, "but you sure can't fool them circle flies because they know an asshole when they see one."

This last joke is one of my favorites; it is what I call a timeless joke because it shows just how bull-headed a person can become when they live alone too long. This story took place when a farmer's horse got the colic. Since the farmer, Harry, didn't know how to treat the animal, he flagged down another farmer as he was passing the farm. Known as Luke, this passerby was a loner and a man of few words who, it was rumoured, knew lots about animals. When asked to stop, Luke shouted, "Whoa."

"Luke, my horse has the colic; what did you give your horse when

155

he had the colic?"

"Turpentine; giddap."

Two weeks later Harry was working in the fields when he spotted Luke going by so he flagged him down and said, "Say, Luke, I gave my horse turpentine like you said and it killed him."

Back came the reply, "Killed mine too, giddap."

And that's enough of Hap's humour.

My final thought on the Bowdens concerns an event that took place recently while I was visiting them with pilot Don Redden. Near the end of the interview Hap got into a story about bygone days, the content of which has slipped my mind. But I do recall that when he finished the story he added, "I know there has to be a supreme power somewhere and I sure hope to shake his hand someday."

Instantly I held out my hand and said, "Okay, put her there."

Hap responded by grabbing my hand and shaking it vigorously for at least a minute, and then after the laughter died down, he held up his hands and exclaimed, "Now I've done absolutely everything!"